CREATING RESILIENT FINANCIAL REGIMES IN ASIA: CHALLENGES AND POLICY OPTIONS

Proceedings of an
Asian Development Bank Seminar
Manila, 29 April 1996

Edited by
Priya Basu

Published for the Asian Development Bank
by Oxford University Press

HONG KONG
OXFORD UNIVERSITY PRESS
OXFORD NEW YORK
1997

Oxford University Press

Oxford New York
Athens Auckland Bangkok Bogota Bombay
Buenos Aires Calcutta Cape Town Dar es Salaam
Delhi Florence Hong Kong Istanbul Karachi
Kuala Lumpur Madras Madrid Melbourne
Mexico City Nairobi Paris Singapore
Taipei Tokyo Toronto Warsaw

and associated companies in
Berlin Ibadan

Oxford is a trade mark of Oxford University Press

First published 1997
This impression (lowest digit)
1 3 5 7 9 10 8 6 4 2

Published for the Asian Development Bank by
Oxford University Press

British Library Cataloguing in Publication Data
available

Library of Congress Cataloging-in-Publication Data

ISBN 0-19-590440-0

Creating Resilient Financial Regimes in Asia: Challenges and Policy Options
edited by Priya Basu
p. cm.
"Papers and proceedings of a seminar organized by the Asian Development Bank"
ISBN 0-19-590440-0
1. Monetary policy —Asia—Congresses. 2. Finance —Asia—Congresses. I. Basu, Priya,1966-   .
II. Asian Development Bank.

HG1202.T68 1997   97-20112
332.4'95-dc21   CIP

Printed in Hong Kong
Published by Oxford University Press (China) Ltd
18/F Warwick House, Taikoo Place, 979 King's Road,
Quarry Bay, Hong Kong

CONTENTS

Chapter Eight
Conclusions and Summing-up   159
Roberto de Ocampo

Figures

Tables

CONTRIBUTORS

Priya Basu
Economist, Financial Sector and Industry Division,
Infrastructure, Energy and Financial Sectors Department (East),
Asian Development Bank, Manila

Marian Bond
Financial Sector Consultant

Donald T. Brash
Governor, Reserve Bank of New Zealand

Paul M. Dickie
Director, Infrastructure, Energy and Financial
Sectors Department (East),
Asian Development Bank, Manila

Soedradjad Djiwandono
Governor, Bank Indonesia

E.V.K. FitzGerald
Director, Finance and Trade Policy Research Center,
International Development Center,
Queen Elizabeth House, Oxford University

Morris Goldstein
Dennis Weatherstone Senior Fellow, Institute of
International Economics, Washington, D.C.

Li Ruogu
Executive Director for the People's Republic of China,
Asian Development Bank, Manila

Ronald I. McKinnon
William Eberly Professor of International Economics,
Stanford University

Roberto de Ocampo
Secretary of Finance, Republic of the Philippines

ABBREVIATIONS

ADB	Asian Development Bank
BI	Bank Indonesia
BIS	Bank for International Settlements
Cetes	Mexican Government peso-denominated bonds
ERM	European Exchange Rate Mechanism
EMU	European Monetary Union
FDICIA	Federal Deposit Insurance Corporation Improvement Act (of the United States)
GAB	General Agreements to Borrow
GDP	Gross Domestic Product
GNP	Gross National Product
IMF	International Monetary Fund
NCD	Negotiable Certificates of Deposit
NOP	New Open Position (regulation in Indonesia)
OECD	Organisation for Economic Co-operation and Development
PBC	People's Bank of China
PPP	Purchasing Power Parity
PRC	People's Republic of China
RBNZ	Reserve Bank of New Zealand
RMB	Renminbi
SOE	State-Owned Enterprise
Tesobonos	Mexican Government dollar-indexed bonds
TVE	Township and Village Enterprise
UK	United Kingdom
USA	United States of America

FOREWORD

Asia's overwhelming economic achievements over the past several decades and the scope and speed of the region's success have captured the imagination of economists and business people the world over. Yet, the basic ingredients of that success are relatively simple: high domestic savings rates and the ability to channel savings toward productive investments. Asia's capacity to mobilize and direct its deep pool of savings toward the most dynamic economic growth sectors has served the region well until now and will no doubt continue to do so in the future.

In recent years, the region's rapidly growing investment needs for infrastructure have increasingly exceeded the financing capability of its governments. This financing challenge has become formidable at a time when official flows from abroad are becoming more scarce. Critical private sector financing is being sought, therefore, from both domestic and foreign sources.

Over the past decade, the growth in private capital inflows to Asia has been remarkable: aggregate net long-term private capital flows increased twentyfold between 1987 and 1995. This trend should not, however, make Asia complacent. In looking to the private sector to finance the region's rapidly growing infrastructure needs, much more has to be done to generate the long-term debt required to match readily available foreign capital. Asian economies must strive not only to improve their already high rates of success in mobilizing domestic resources, but also to channel more of these resources into longer term commitments through the newly emerging debt markets. To achieve this, significant changes will be required in Asian equity and debt markets, as well as in commercial banks—which are the basic building blocks of Asia's financial systems.

Over the last 30 years, the Asian Development Bank (ADB) has played a catalytic role in mobilizing and allocating financial resources for development in Asia through efforts focused on banking sector development, the strengthening of nonbank financial institutions, and the development and deepening of capital markets—both equity markets and markets for long-term debt. The main objective of ADB's operations in the financial sector has been to create stable, competitive, market-based financial systems that are able to mobilize and allocate domestic resources in an efficient and effective manner. Stronger domestic financial sectors will place the economies of the Asian region in a better position to raise foreign capital in the future.

There is, of course, an immense variation in the levels of development within Asia and, consequently, in the demands placed on domestic financial systems. As a regional development bank, ADB is ideally positioned to provide solutions sensitive to the particular needs of its borrowing members. In the transition economies of Asia, ADB has focused mainly on building market-based banking systems. This involves promoting commercialization and competition in the banking system, improving the credit analysis of banks, introducing international standards to improve the capital adequacy of banks, and enhancing banking supervision. In 1996, ADB provided such assistance to Lao People's Democratic Republic, Mongolia, and Socialist Republic of Viet Nam.

In the higher income, emerging market economies of East and Southeast Asia, and also to a certain extent in South Asia, as financial sectors have been liberalized, the role of capital markets has increased in importance. ADB's financial sector operations in these emerging market economies thus focus mainly on developing capital markets and nonbank financial institutions, particularly with a view to assisting these economies in meeting their long-term financial resource needs. The emphasis is on enhancing market regulation and supervision, improving transparency and stability, reducing systemic risk, and developing the necessary market infrastructure. Such assistance has been provided to People's Republic of China (PRC), India, Republic of Indonesia, and Republic of the Philippines, among other countries. For example, ADB technical assistance to the PRC has helped to establish an automated securities trading system and to improve the capacity of the country's Securities Regulatory Commission. ADB is also currently assisting the PRC in developing a modern payments system. ADB's capital market loans to India and the Philippines have played an important role in deepening capital markets. Financial sector program loans to Indonesia have supported an enhanced regulatory framework for the country's stock market and have strengthened debt markets. ADB has also participated in the development of investment funds for the region, such as the Asian Infrastructure Fund.

To contribute to a better understanding of the challenges and policy options related to financial sector development in Asia, ADB organized, on the occasion of the Twenty-ninth Annual Meeting of its Board of Governors, a high-level seminar on *Financial Sector in Transition*. The Seminar brought together a group of eminent policy makers, financial sector practitioners, and scholars. The presentations made at the Seminar and the discussions that followed have helped shape a vision for the development of Asia's financial sector. This book, which contains the edited papers and proceedings of the Seminar, captures that vision.

Peter H. Sullivan
Vice-President, Region East

PREFACE

Financial reform and the subsequent management and regulation of the financial sector are key aspects of economic policy in Asia's emerging market economies. Over the past decade or so, a large number of economies throughout Asia have taken steps toward deepening their financial systems, by deregulating domestic financial markets and establishing closer links between domestic and international capital markets. While financial reform experiments in a number of Asian countries have met with a great deal of success, for most Asian countries, much remains to be done in creating financial regimes that are more flexible and resilient when confronted with domestic and external shocks.

To contribute to a better understanding of the main challenges, constraints, and policy options with respect to financial reform in Asia, the Asian Development Bank (ADB) organized a high-level seminar in April 1996 on financial sector development in Asia. The seminar, which brought together a panel of very distinguished policy makers, scholars, and financial sector practitioners, provided a forum for the exchange of ideas and information on policy, institutional, legal, and regulatory issues related to the financial sector. The focus of the seminar was on reforms in banking and capital markets, and on associated macroeconomic policy adjustments required in the context of an increasingly open financial sector. The opening address was delivered by Roberto de Ocampo, Finance Secretary of the Philippines, who chaired the seminar and also provided a summing-up at the end. The past efforts and the future challenges relative to financial reform in Republic of Indonesia, People's Republic of China (PRC), and New Zealand were examined, respectively, by Soedradjad Djiwandono, Governor of Bank Indonesia; Li Ruogu, Executive Director for the PRC at ADB; and Donald T. Brash, Governor of the Reserve Bank of New Zealand. The country presentations highlighted differences in the content, pace, and sequencing of financial reforms in these countries, and different perceptions on the optimal order of financial liberalization. These were followed by comments from three leading scholars—Ronald McKinnon, William Eberly Professor of International Economics at Stanford University, USA; Morris Goldstein, Dennis Weatherstone Senior Fellow at the Institute of International Economics, Washington, D.C., USA; and E.V.K. FitzGerald, Director, Finance and Trade Policy Research Center, International Development Center, Queen Elizabeth House, Oxford University, UK—who, in their role as discussants, reflected on the country experiences in a wider context.

This book contains the edited papers and proceedings of the Seminar. The book was edited by Priya Basu, Economist, Financial Sector and Industry Division (East) at ADB. Excellent editorial advice was provided by Marian E. Bond, Financial Sector Consultant. Lyle Raquipiso and Ma. Josephine Duque extended editorial assistance. Many people, inside ADB and outside it, made valuable contributions to the completion of this book. Charles F. Coe, Manager, Financial Sector and Industry Division (East), provided very useful comments at various stages during the preparation of this book. Lynette Mallery of the Information Office put in many hours of work in coordinating the publishing of this book with Oxford University Press. Raveendranath Rajan, Head, Contracts and Printing Section at ADB, coordinated the printing, and Vic Angeles designed the cover. Rose Arcano did the typesetting. Yolanda Arcinas provided technical assistance in dealing with administrative matters. Jennifer Canapi and Cheche Lorena provided secretarial assistance. And finally, ADB would like to express its deep appreciation to the very distinguished outside panelists for their invaluable insights into financial sector policy and institutional issues, and for agreeing to allow us to publish their contributions in this book.

The views and opinions expressed in this book are those of the individual authors and do not necessarily represent the views of the Asian Development Bank.

PAUL M. DICKIE
Director, Infrastructure, Energy and
Financial Sectors Department (East)

CHAPTER ONE

FINANCIAL REFORM IN ASIA: AN OVERVIEW

PRIYA BASU

Financial reform, and the subsequent management and regulation of the sector, have been accorded a central position in the economic reform programs of economies throughout Asia. Over the past decade or so, a large number of Asian economies have taken steps toward developing market-based financial systems that are better equipped to mobilize financial resources and channel these resources into productive investments in an efficient manner. East and Southeast Asia's success in this respect is particularly noteworthy; other Asian economies are now making efforts to follow suit. In economies throughout the region, including East and Southeast Asian economies with their already high savings rate, there is a growing thirst for long-term capital, as rapidly growing needs for infrastructure investment are beginning to outrun the financing capabilities of governments and official sources of finance.[1] This financing challenge is indeed for-

---

[1] Estimates of the region's future infrastructure investment demands vary widely. One estimate, based on a calculation by the Asian Development Bank, suggests that for the whole of non-Japanese Asia, the demand for infrastructure investment over the period 1991-2000 will amount to around US$1 trillion (US$350 billion for transport, another US$350 billion for power, US$150 billion for telecommunications, and US$100 billion for water supply and sanitation). The World Bank projects that between US$1.2 to 1.5 trillion will be neeeded for the period 1995-2004 to finance infrastructure investment in East Asian and the Pacific Island developing countries.

midable, and underscores the urgent need for strengthening reform efforts to deepen financial systems and build more resilient financial regimes—encompassing the banking sector and capital markets—that are better able to serve the region's financing needs.

It should be emphasized at the very outset that generalizations about Asia need to be treated with caution. The analysis presented in this chapter will exclude Japan, home of the world's biggest (and currently, most debt-troubled) banks, on the ground that Japan's financial markets are developed; the financial reform that is still to come in Japan will affect its markets only at the margin rather than fundamentally. But even in developing Asia, there is an immense variety in the form and extent of financial reform undertaken so far and, consequently, in the demands being placed on financial systems across countries.

Differences in financial reform experiences across developing Asia may be attributed, at least in part, to differences in initial conditions that, in turn, have affected the overall design and scope of the reform programs implemented. In broad terms, developing Asian economies may be classified into two groups in terms of their initial conditions and subsequent financial reform programs: on the one hand, the more "mature" economies of East Asia, Southeast Asia, and South Asia that embarked on reforms in the 1970s and the 1980s, and on the other hand, the "transition" (former command) economies of Asia, where financial reforms were generally initiated in the early 1990s.

Economies in both groups tended to be characterized by intensive government intervention in their financial sectors when they embarked on their reform programs.[2] However, the East, Southeast, and South Asian economies generally had more diversified financial systems, even prior to reforms, than the transition economies. In the latter, former command, economies of Asia, financial sectors generally comprised a single state-owned bank (or monobank), which acted as the expenditure arm of the Treasury, allocating financial resources according to government directives and controlling money supply through direct intervention. Financial reforms in the majority of these transition

---

[2] The exceptions being Hong Kong and the Republic of Singapore, where government intervention was insignificant.

economies, initiated in the early 1990s, have been implemented rapidly—often dubbed the "big bang" approach. A notable exception is the People's Republic of China (PRC), which initiated reforms in the early 1980s and where reforms have been gradual. Among the East, Southeast, and South Asian economies, the four East Asian economies of Hong Kong, Republic of Korea, Singapore, and Taipei,China were the earliest to embark on financial reforms (starting as early as the 1970s), followed by the Southeast Asian economies of the Republic of Indonesia, Malaysia, Kingdom of Thailand, and Republic of the Philippines (although Indonesia introduced some reforms in the 1970s). These economies have, in general, met with considerable success in reforming their financial sectors to create diversified and competitive financial sectors; the task ahead for these countries is mainly one of consolidating the reform process and deepening the financial sectors. In contrast, progress with financial reform in South Asia has been relatively slower and the reform challenge is consequently greater. And for most transition economies, the task of creating market-based financial systems is still enormous.

This chapter provides an introductory overview of the past efforts and future challenges with respect to financial reform in Asia, setting the stage for the discussion in subsequent chapters of this volume. The chapter begins by presenting an analysis of the theoretical and empirical underpinnings of the relationship between financial sector development, savings, and economic growth, highlighting, in particular, the role of well-developed financial systems in promoting economic growth. It then examines reforms undertaken in the banking sector and money markets, as well as equity and debt markets, presenting an assessment of the current state of financial and capital market development in Asia and the challenges confronting the region with respect to creating more resilient financial regimes.

FINANCIAL SECTOR DEVELOPMENT, SAVINGS, AND ECONOMIC GROWTH: THEORY AND EVIDENCE FROM ASIA

A common goal of developing countries is to achieve high and sustained economic growth. There has been much debate among academics over how such growth can be achieved. At the center of this debate lie two sharply differing perspectives on the role of financial markets in promoting economic growth: the "forced-saving" approach and the "prior-saving" approach.[3]

According to the Keynesian forced-savings school, finance is viewed as merely the handmaiden of industry, responding positively to other factors that determine growth; it is investment that is the constraining factor for growth. Prior savings and financial development are not seen as a requirement for investment and growth, and investment, it is believed, can be increased autonomously by the government (without prior saving) through monetary expansion. Further, such an investment, they argue, would generate its own savings. According to this view, since investment, not saving, is the constraint to growth, a low or negative real interest rate is necessary for encouraging private investment. To the extent that a high rate of inflation keeps the real interest rate low, inflation is seen as a necessary price of economic development. A key policy implication following from this school of thought involved government intervention to keep nominal interest rates at levels below the market rate, often resulting in low or negative real interest rates.

Thus, during the heyday of the Keynesian revolution in the 1950s and 1960s, the importance of financial factors in economic growth was largely ignored. Under the influence of the forced-savings school, in many developing countries in Asia, as well as elsewhere, financial intermediaries were subject to a plethora of controls. Interest rates on deposits and loans were determined by government directives. Financial institutions were often required to lend to the central government and other public sec-

---

[3] For a critical and detailed discussion on the major approaches to development finance, see Khatkhate (1972), Thirlwall (1989), and Hossain and Chowdhury (1996).

tor entities at below-market interest rates, or to provide foreign exchange at official exchange rates that overvalued domestic currency for public sector debt-service payments or for imports by state-owned enterprises. Governments also tended to raise revenues implicitly by requiring commercial banks to hold underremunerated reserves with the central bank or by requiring foreign exchange proceeds of commodity exports to be repatriated at below-market exchange rates for foreign currency. All these policies have been collectively referred to as *financial repression*.

Since the early 1970s, the view that repressive financial policies raise investment and accelerate economic growth has come under much criticism from the prior-saving school, notably from the seminal works of McKinnon (1973) and Shaw (1973),[4] and this has driven many countries in the region to move toward market-oriented financial systems. Advocates of the prior-saving school challenge the view that repressive financial policies raise investment and accelerate economic growth. They argue that financial markets play a key role in economic activity, and that saving is the constraining factor for growth. Prior savings are seen as the determinant of investment, and all savings find their investment outlets. Proponents of this view are averse to inflation, and do not see the need for inflation for growth. Because investment is an alternative to consumption, this view argues that investment that is not financed by prior savings will generate inflation but no real income. Savings and financial development are thus seen as key elements in economic development. The policy implication following from this view favors financial liberalization (characterized by market-determined interest rates), which is believed to enhance the aggregate savings rate, induce financial deepening, and improve investment efficiency. These salutary effects in turn contribute to economic growth. The role of monetary policy in developing countries, according to this view, should be to mobilize savings, and channel savings into productive investment by keeping the inflation rate low so that the real interest rate remains positive over time.

---

[4] Also see McKinnon (1989).

Recent theoretical and empirical research also suggests that financial markets play an important role in economic growth. Well-developed financial systems can promote growth in a number of ways: first, by evaluating investment projects and their sponsoring entrepreneurs; second, by raising savings to fund selected projects; and third, by promoting the diversification of risks.[5] It seems clear that better financial systems stimulate productivity, growth, and higher income levels. Findings suggest that government policies to promote enhanced financial systems will promote long-term growth.[6]

Cross-country data for a sample of seven East and Southeast Asian economies presented in Figure 1.1 show that economies that have enjoyed a higher level of financial development, as measured by the assets and liabilities of the banking sectors, have also tended to experience faster GDP growth. These economies are also at higher levels of economic development, as indicated by higher levels of GDP per capita, and savings ratios in all these countries (with the exception of the Philippines and Taipei,China) are currently above 30 percent of GDP.

The data in Figure 1.1.1 show that countries such as PRC, the Republic of Korea, Malaysia, and Thailand, characterized by more developed financial systems, as measured by the ratio of financial liabilities to GDP, have tended to have the highest GDP growth; the correlation coefficient is 0.67. The same countries also have high ratios of financial assets to GDP, as shown in Figure 1.1.2, with a correlation coefficient of 0.51.

Moreover, the experience of these economies points to the existence of a virtuous circle encompassing economic growth and the level of financial development, where the latter is tightly linked to a country's potential growth. Not only has growth been spurred by the greater availability of capital made possible by financial development, but also the development of the financial sector has itself been driven by economic growth, high income, and saving.

However, not all economies in the region have experienced virtuous circles of financial sector development, savings, and eco-

---

[5] On the question of the role of efficient financial markets in pooling risks and facilitating transactions, see Stiglitz (1994).

[6] King and Levine (1993b). Also see King and Levine (1993a).

Figure 1.1   Financial Development and Economic Growth in Selected Developing Economies, 1990-1995 Average

Figure 1.1.1

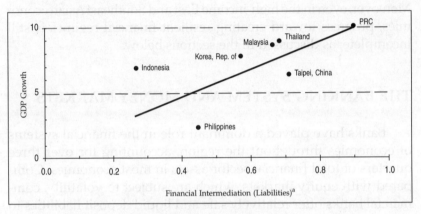

a The ratio of commercial bank liabilities to GDP.

Figure 1.1.2

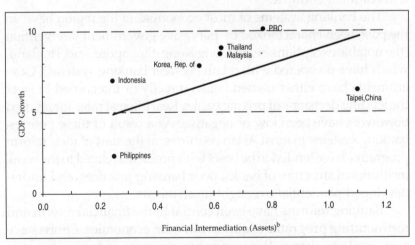

b The ratio of nongovernment credit from commercial banks to GDP.

nomic growth. Growth rates in many of the transition economies of Asia as well as in South Asian economies have lagged behind. Despite efforts over the last decade directed at financial reform, the financial sectors of many of these economies remain beset with a number of problems that impede the efficient functioning of their banking systems, and capital markets remain underdeveloped. Moreover, even in the high-income East and Southeast Asian economies, progress toward creating resilient financial regimes is still incomplete, as discussed in the sections below.

THE BANKING SYSTEM AND MONEY MARKETS

Banks have played a dominant role in the financial systems of economies throughout the region, accounting for over three quarters of total financial sector assets in most economies. Compared with equity markets, which are subject to volatility, commercial banks offer relatively safe and liquid deposit liabilities to savers and therefore constitute the major resource mobilization network. Banks also remain the single largest lender to the corporate sector. The banking sector's role has been further reinforced by the central position it has occupied in the payment systems of most countries.

The banking systems of most economies in the region have, in the past, been characterized by pervasive government intervention (the notable exceptions being Hong Kong, Singapore, and Thailand, which have prospered with relatively freer banking systems). Governments have either owned banks directly or intervened to steer the lending decisions of private banks. Real interest rates for favored borrowers have been low or negative. As a result of these policies, banking systems in most Asian countries, at the start of their reform programs, have tended to be beset with problems related to the weak institutional structure of banks, poor banking practices, and underdeveloped prudential oversight mechanisms.

Banking reforms have been central to the financial reform and restructuring programs of almost all Asian economies. Efforts have been made to change the ownership structure of banks, open up banking sectors to domestic private as well as foreign competition, commercialize banking practices, expand the range of services, and improve regulatory oversight of banks. Nevertheless, a number of problems persist in the banking sectors of the economies in the region—albeit in varying degrees.

Institutional Reforms

As regards institutional reforms, a major source of difficulty has been that reforms that gave financial markets and institutions greater freedom were often not supported by sufficient efforts to break out of the legacy of control and protection that characterized the banking systems of many countries in Asia during the 1960s and 1970s. An important element of this unsatisfactory structure has been banking inefficiency.

Economies throughout the region tended to be characterized by inefficient banking sectors when they embarked on their reform efforts. Large state-owned banks had traditionally played a dominant role in the banking systems. With loan policies subject to government direction or other forms of political pressure, banks did not always evaluate credit risks properly. They could also afford to be overstaffed and maintain excessive branch networks.

A banking system can become more efficient only if liberalization is accompanied by measures to enable the more competitive banks to absorb and reform the weaker banks or to allow new entrants to drive out incompetent banks. Yet, in many economies, the takeover mechanism has frequently been obstructed by various restrictions that have remained in force through the reform process. A number of economies have also retained restrictions on the entry of new banks, especially foreign banks. In India, Taipei,China, and Thailand, for example, new banking licenses are being granted for the first time in years. For many countries, the oligopolistic banking structure that has often survived reform efforts has served to stifle competition.

In addition, reforms have not always led to the privatization of state banks, whose share in total banking sector assets remains high for some economies in the region, notably for India and Indonesia. In contrast, economies such as Hong Kong and Singapore, and also the Republic of Korea, Malaysia, and Thailand, have followed vigorous privatization programs and only a small portion of their financial sectors now remains under public control (in the case of Hong Kong and Singapore, the share of state-owned banks in total assets is zero). In this context, a no-

table exception among the region's high-income East Asian economies is Taipei,China, where most banking remains under public
control, but here, too, the government is permitting some entry
and expansion of new domestic and foreign banks (Table 1.1).

In those economies that have undertaken more far-reaching
reforms in their banking sectors, it is difficult to assess the extent
to which these reforms have made banks more efficient in providing services, and the time taken to achieve this change. In its Annual Report for 1996, the Bank for International Settlements (BIS)
has considered one measure that can approximate the cost of in-

**Table 1.1   Indicators of the Efficiency of the Banking
Industry**

Economy	Share of State-owned Banks (percentage share of assets) 1994	Operating Costs (percent of total assets) 1990-1994	Net Interest Margins (percent of total assets) 1990-1994	Deposits in the Central Bank as a Percent of Loans to Nongovernment Sector		Average Inflation Rates 1990-1994
				1994	1995	
Hong Kong	0	0.8	1.6	0.1	0.1	n.a.
Korea, Rep. of	13	1.7	2.1	7.5	7.9	6.6
Singapore	0	1.4	1.6	6.7	6.5	2.8
Taipei,China	57	1.3	2.0	9.9	8.7	n.a.
Indonesia	48	2.4	3.3	0.5	1.1	8.8
Malaysia	8	1.6	3.0	0.0	0.2	4.1
Thailand	7	1.9	3.7	1.2	1.4	4.6
India	87	2.3	2.9	21.3	15.6	10.5
Germany	50	1.1	1.4	1.7	1.3	5.6
Japan	0	0.8	1.1	0.6	0.6	1.7

Source: Bank for International Settlements (1996).

termediation by banks, which is the net interest margin. Although
this is an imperfect indicator, particularly for international com-
parisons of the efficiency of banks, nevertheless, international com-
parisons show a similarity between net interest margins and operating costs for many Asian economies, suggesting that cross-country differences in interest margins reflect differences in banking
efficiency, rather than payment for different risks (Table 1.1).

Using these measurements, banks in the emerging Asian markets fall roughly into two broad groups. The first group comprises banks in the high-income East Asian economies of Hong Kong, the Republic of Korea, Singapore, and Taipei,China, which, for the years 1990 to 1994 had an average net interest margin of between 1.6 and 2.1 percent of total assets, not that much above the margins in Germany and Japan of 1.4 and 1.1, respectively. The higher income East Asian economies also have the lowest operating costs, measuring between 1.3 and 1.7 percent of total assets; these, too, are close to the operating costs in developed countries.

The second group consists of banks in other Asian countries, including India, Indonesia, Malaysia, and Thailand, where average net interest margins of between 3 and 4 percent of total assets have been calculated, with corresponding operating costs of between 1.9 and 2.4 percent of total assets.

It is difficult to make a conclusive judgment on banking efficiency across countries, based on measurements of net interest margin, because differences in net interest margins could be a reflection of differences in inflation across countries. However, cross-country patterns observed here suggest that inflation was not a key determinant in differences in net interest margins, as a percentage of total assets. In other words, the evidence suggests that much of the cross-country difference in interest margins reflects differing levels of banking system efficiency rather than payment for different risks.

Reform of Banking Practices

A second area of focus with respect to reforming the banking systems in economies of the region has been banking practices. While reforms to improve banking practices have included efforts to diversify bank assets, reduce lending to connected enterprises, correct mismatches between assets and liabilities, and value collateral more accurately, progress in each of these areas has been slow and uneven across countries.

The inadequate diversification of bank assets has been a central failing of the banking systems of many economies in the region. Specialist banks have been overdependent on the particular sector/ area served, and this problem is particularly significant for the transition economies.

Another weakness has been a concentration on loans for real estate, or indeed any other long-term investment project. The problem with using bank finance for a long-term project is that its present value is typically very sensitive to changes in the rate of interest. In recognition of the potential problems in this context, a number of economies have taken steps in recent years to impose limits on real estate loans. For example, a recent guideline issued by Hong Kong encourages banks with a property exposure of more than 40 percent of loans to reduce or stabilize the proportion. Furthermore, small economies, with exports concentrated on only a few commodities, may offer banks limited scope for diversification. In such circumstances, a resilient banking system that is insulated from domestic shocks can only be created through international diversification.

Another practice that has characterized the banking systems of many economies in the region, and has persisted in the case of many transition economies, countries of South Asia and even East Asia (for example, the Republic of Korea) and Southeast Asia involves lending to connected enterprises (for example, industrial enterprises, which have a major stake in the bank). This has often compromised objective risk assessment.

In a number of economies in the region, banking is characterized by excessive maturity and currency mismatches between assets and liabilities. Where bank finance is practically the only source of investment finance, even for long-term projects, as it is in a number of economies, banks whose funds are drawn from short-term deposits face potentially serious maturity mismatches. When interest rates are freed up, banks lose the protection of the controlled structure that typically kept short-term rates below long-term rates. Attempts by banks to avoid this interest rate risk by charging their long-term borrowers variable interest rates (linked to short-term rates) may rebound on them as a credit risk if their customers face servicing difficulties when short-term interest rates rise sharply.

There is also often a temptation to overvalue collateral, particularly during an economic upswing. A related issue is the importance of ensuring that loan-to-value ratios of mortgages reflect the risk that property prices can fall. Furthermore, in a number of economies, it is difficult to collect on collateral because of poorly developed legal systems.

Prudential Oversight

The banking systems of many economies in Asia have been characterized by the absence of adequate prudential oversight that is necessary to cope with the problems of increased risk, asymmetric information, and moral hazard that are almost inevitably associated with more liberalized, market-oriented financial systems.

In recent years, many Asian economies have taken steps to strengthen their systems of prudential oversight to cope with these increased risks. Particularly significant prudential rules include those related to limits on the entry of new institutions, capital/asset ratios, and auditing and accounting standards.

In general, Asian economies have been cautious in permitting new entrants in the banking sector. Notable exceptions include Hong Kong and Indonesia. Hong Kong lifted its moratorium on new bank licenses in 1978; however, the banking crisis in 1982 led to a significant tightening of restrictions. Indonesia has made rapid progress in terms of ease of entry for domestic and foreign banks, starting in the late 1980s, when the Indonesian banking sector was opened to entry by privately owned and foreign-owned banks and the expansion of private banks was encouraged. Part of its banking is still, however, in state banks. In the transition economies, governments have started to decentralize their banking functions; the PRC, for example, has introduced a degree of competition into its financial sector by commercializing some of the operations of state-owned banks and opening up the banking sector to foreign banks. (This is discussed in greater detail in Chapter Three.) The widespread restrictions on entry in South Asia have also slowly started to change, though most banking assets remain in government banks. In the People's Republic of Bangladesh and India, restrictions on the entry of foreign banks into the market have been eased.

The most prominent capital/asset rule is the 8 percent capital adequacy ratio laid down by the Basle Committee on Banking Supervision. While almost all the East and Southeast Asian economies have adopted this risk-based capital adequacy standard, practice in most other economies in the region has moved only slowly toward reflecting the spirit of this regulation. Equally, measures of capital depend on accurate accounting. Yet, accounting and auditing standards are often lax and ill-defined.

Furthermore, in most economies of the region, oversight has traditionally been characterized by governments controlling and managing markets and participants. Under this approach, regulatory and supervisory responsibilities tend to be entirely assumed by the authorities. However, officially enforced rules and regulations can only be a part of any oversight mechanism; disclosure and market-based control mechanisms have an essential role to play in ensuring efficiency. In this context, New Zealand's experiment with market-based reforms in banking regulation and supervision (discussed in Chapter Five) is of particular relevance. Disclosure and market-based regulation and supervision are especially necessary in the face of rapidly changing financial market structures. The Indonesian experience in the late 1980s (examined in detail in Chapter Four) provides interesting insights into this issue.

Money Markets

Money markets transfer short-term funds through financial intermediaries to those in need of funds. Thus, they provide financial intermediaries and other businesses with a flexible means of managing short-term liquidity. They also provide an indirect instrument of monetary policy. Furthermore, money markets can provide a benchmark for market-based interest rates. Interbank markets have generally led the way in most East and Southeast Asian economies. A range of short-term instruments such as certificates of deposits and commercial paper have been developed.

Singapore and Hong Kong have the most developed money markets in the region. In Hong Kong, the money market in the form of Hong Kong dollar interbank deposits is an important source of short-term funding for the banking sector. In addition, the markets for commercial paper and negotiable certificates of deposit (NCD) have been active since the 1970s, although the interbank market is almost ten times the size of the NCD market. Singapore's domestic money market comprises two closely linked markets: the interbank and discount markets. In the interbank market, surplus funds are placed with those in need of funds for periods ranging from overnight placements to placements for 12 months. In the discount market, short-term money market instruments are issued, traded, and discounted. However, formal money market instruments, including treasury bills, commercial bills, and Singapore dollar NCDs, still account for only a small proportion of money market transactions.

CAPITAL MARKETS

At the time they embarked on financial reform programs, most economies in the region had no significant capital markets (equity and bond markets) to speak of; financial intermediation centered on, and around, the banking system. Over the last decade or so, many economies in the region, and particularly those in East and Southeast Asia, have made efforts to develop capital markets. As capital markets have begun to take off, commercial banks are beginning to face new competitive pressures: if companies can borrow direct from capital markets and investors can put their money direct into the stock market, banks lose their traditional role of middleman between borrowers and lenders. Such "disintermediation" has already begun to drive down the quantity of bank loans in economies with more developed capital markets, for example, Singapore (Table 1.2). It may also drive down the quality of bank loans, because the most creditworthy companies can tap the capital markets themselves. Furthermore, as capital markets develop, depositors may also turn elsewhere— for example, to mutual funds, which offer higher returns than banks. (The phenomenon of financial disintermediation is discussed in greater detail in Chapter Two.)

The Growth of Equity Markets

A number of economies have made great strides over the last decade toward establishing and invigorating equity markets, mainly as a result of strong economic growth coupled with concerted government efforts to foster equity market development.

As a ratio of GNP, equity market capitalization (which reflects the extent to which equity markets are able to mobilize capital) in Malaysia and Singapore has exceeded the figure for the United States, and in economies such as Thailand, Philippines, and Taipei,China, the ratios of market capitalization to GNP are close to industrial country averages (Table 1.3). Likewise, liquidity has not been a cause for concern in these East and Southeast

Table 1.2   Comparative Financial Market Indicators,
as Percent of GDP

Economy	Equity Market[a]		Bond Market[b]		Bank Assets		M2	
	1990	1995	1990	1995	1990	1995	1990	1995
Hong Kong	111.5	211.4	1.3	10.2	n.a.	n.a.	207.7	203.8
Korea, Rep. of	44.4	40.2	34.8	41.7	64.9	74.4	38.3	43.8
Singapore	91.8	176.8	68.1	54.4	164.7	158.6	91.3	86.0
Taipei,China	62.3	74.0	n.a.	n.a.	n.a.	n.a.	144.7	182.9
PRC	n.a.	6.1	6.7	6.8	104.7	113.6	79.2	105.2
Indonesia	7.2	34.2	1.6	4.3	57.8	n.a.	40.1	50.0
Malaysia	113.4	264.7	63.3	52.4	95.9	114.7	66.3	92.7
Philippines	15.0	81.0	19.6	32.4	45.0	64.6	34.1	50.4
Thailand	27.7	85.6	9.9	10.1	78.4	115.1	69.9	79.5
Japan	99.5	71.8	72.2	73.7[c]	164.1	157.3	116.6	114.2
United States	55.4	94.6	94.1	110.2[c]	53.8	51.0	68.2	58.5

[a]   Size of equity market based on total capitalization in local currency as a
percentage of GDP in local currency.
[b]   Size of bond market based on value of total bonds outstanding in local
currency as a percentage of GDP in local currency.
[c]   Japan and US figures on size of bond market refer to 1994 figures.

Sources: 1. Emerging Asian Bond Market, World Bank (Washington, D.C.: 1996).
2. Emerging Stock Markets Factbook 1996, International Finance
Corporation (Washington, D.C.: 1996).
3. Washington Asset Management Inc., 1996.
4. International Financial Statistics Yearbook 1996, International Monetary Fund (Washington, D.C.: 1996).
5. Key Indicators of Developing Asian and Pacific Countries 1996,
Asian Development Bank (Manila: 1996).

Asian economies, as turnover rates have been in excess of 25 percent with markets in the Republic of Korea, Taipei,China, and
PRC even demonstrating higher rates than those in the United
States. On the other hand, there has been considerable market
concentration, with the 10 largest companies holding more than
30 percent of market capitalization in a number of countries of
the region. This can adversely affect the liquidity of the market.
Furthermore, in other economies of the region, turnover is still
relatively low and is dominated by transactions in the shares of a
few large companies. Price volatility is often higher in emerging
Asian economies than in industrial countries.

Table 1.3   Comparative Stock Market Indicators for 11 Asia-Pacific Economies

Indicator	Hong Kong	Republic of Korea	Singapore	Taipei, China	PRC	Indonesia	Malaysia	Philippines	Thailand	Japan	USA
Market capitalization (US$ billion)	303.71	181.96	148.00	187.21	42.06	66.59	222.73	58.86	141.51	3,667.29	6,857.62
Growth of market capitalization, 1991-1995 (%)	36.90	18.40	46.40	19.10	231.60	83.60	49.20	67.80	48.80	6.10	14.60
Market capitalization/GNP, 1995	n.a.	40.50	175.60	73.20	6.10	35.80	279.40	78.30	87.60	n.a.	94.80
IFCG total return index, 1994-1995 (percentage change)	n.a.	-5.70	n.a.	-30.70	-12.40	12.00	3.60	-14.10	-1.40	n.a.	n.a.
Value traded, 1995 (US$ billion)	106.89	185.20	60.46	383.10	49.77	14.40	76.82	14.73	57.00	1,231.55	5,108.59
Turnover: average market capitalization divided by total value traded (%)	37.30	97.80	42.20	174.90	115.90	25.30	35.90	26.10	41.40	30.90	85.70
Share of market capitalization held by 10 largest companies, 1995 (%)	n.a.	34.80	n.a.	29.90	20.20	41.30	29.40	39.10	35.90	n.a.	n.a.
Volatility: standard deviation of total return index, 1990-1995	n.a.	7.66	n.a.	11.20	22.03	8.31	6.98	8.90	8.79	n.a.	2.93

Sources: 1. Emerging Stock Markets Factbook 1996, International Finance Corporation (Washington, D.C.: 1996).
2. International Financial Statistics Yearbook 1996, International Monetary Fund (Washington, D.C.: 1996).
3. Key Indicators of Developing Asian and Pacific Countries 1996, Asian Development Bank (Manila: 1996).

Government policy played an important role in promoting equity market development in the Republic of Korea, Malaysia, Singapore, Taipei,China, and Thailand in the mid-1980s, when many of the existing restrictive controls to equity market development were removed and regulations with respect to disclosure and investor protection were strengthened. The Indonesian government has also·made determined efforts to support equity market development. The Jakarta stock market was established in 1977. However, despite a decade of fairly steady growth, there were only 24 companies listed in 1987 and market capitalization was limited. In 1987, the government pushed forth a set of new policies aimed at boosting the stock market: listing requirements were simplified, restrictions on daily price fluctuations were removed, a tax was imposed on bank interest payments, and foreigners were, for the first time, allowed to buy 49 percent of listed companies and set up joint-venture securities firms. The result was a rapid increase in market capitalization. In the Philippines, the Republic of Korea, and Taipei,China, too, efforts have been made to improve the institutional structuring of equity markets and to encourage foreign participation.

While government support is crucial to equity market development, economic growth is also a critical variable in determining market performance. The correlation between growth and rising share prices is not perfect. Speculative booms can raise prices to unsustainable levels. Economic growth can also divert money from stock markets into fixed investment. But, in general, data suggest that fast growing economies will have better performing stock markets. Arguably, the causation can be reversed: by improving the efficiency with which money is channeled from savers to investors, better performing stock markets can, in turn, fuel growth. Companies have new sources of finance; savers have new investment opportunities. Indeed, recent studies on the subject suggest a strong positive correlation between stock market liquidity and economic growth. Among the important factors explaining this relationship is, first, the attractiveness of liquid (as opposed to illiquid) markets to long-term investors, as liquid equity markets allow savers to sell their shares easily while allowing firms access to long-term capital through equity issues; and, second, the fact that liquid stock markets encourage banks to lend, giving investment a further boost.

However, rapid economic growth and government encouragement are not enough to ensure that equity market investments will make money. Much still needs to be done, as discussed below, to improve the regulatory and legal framework governing markets, improve market transparency and disclosure, and strengthen the supporting infrastructure. Many economies in the region still do not have reliable securities laws governing stock market operations. Many stock markets in the region tend to be characterized by wide-scale insider trading. And market infrastructure, including accounting and disclosure systems and trading systems, remains underdeveloped.

The Underdeveloped Nature of Bond Markets

In contrast to equity markets, bond markets in much of the region remain relatively underdeveloped (Table 1.2), although in economies such as Hong Kong, the Republic of Korea, Malaysia, and Singapore, bond markets have begun to take off. Except in Hong Kong and the Republic of Korea, bond issues in most economies in the region are dominated by government bonds, but the secondary markets for such bonds still remain underdeveloped.

Developing bond markets is important because economies throughout the region have an increasing need for long-term capital, particularly to finance infrastructure projects. Government bonds provide economies with a means to raise funds for public expenditures, and serve as benchmark rates for the financial system, allowing more accurate pricing and encouraging the development of other fixed interest securities markets. Corporate bonds, on the other hand, provide an alternative to bank borrowing and equity financing. While corporate bond markets tend to be the least developed segment of the financial system in most economies of the region, since the early 1990s corporate bond markets have shown signs of rapid growth in many economies of the region. The faster growing corporate bond markets have been those in Thailand, Malaysia, the Republic of Korea, and Hong Kong with the Korean market being the largest[7] (see Table 1.4).

---

[7] In essence, however, Korean bond issues are viewed as loan packages in the form of bonds.

Table 1.4   East and Southeast Asian Bond Markets,
as of 1995 (US$ billion)

Economy	National Government	State Government	State Enterprise	Central Bank	Corporate Sector	Total
Hong Kong	0.0	0.0	0.0	7.6	7.0	14.6
Korea, Rep. of	29.9	4.4	43.2	33.3	79.1	190.0
Singapore	43.7	0.0	0.0	0.0	2.6	46.3
PRC	41.4	0.0	4.0	0.0	0.0	45.4
Indonesia	0.0	0.0	2.9	5.2	0.6	8.7
Malaysia	29.2	0.0	4.4	2.4	8.8	44.8
Philippines	23.5	0.0	0.1	0.0	0.5	24.0
Thailand	1.7	0.0	9.5	0.4	5.3	16.8
Total	169.4	4.4	64.1	48.9	103.9	390.6

Source: Dalla, I. "Asian Fixed Income and Currency Session." Presented at the Seminar on The Role of Bond Markets in Infrastructure Investment in Asia, Asian Development Bank, Manila, Philippines, December 6, 1996.

Factors Impeding Capital Market Development

A number of factors have inhibited capital market development, and particularly the development of bond markets, in the region: first, the lack of transparent and credible regulatory and legal systems; second, an inadequately developed market infrastructure, including poor accounting and disclosure standards for business and financial information, the absence of credible and independent credit rating agencies, and the lack of modern and efficient clearing and settlement facilities; and third, the shortage of market-based benchmark rates for medium- to long-term securities.

Regulatory and Legal Framework

Transparent and credible regulatory and legal frameworks are critical to promoting capital market development. Many economies suffer from the lack of a well-developed regulatory framework governing the issuance, trading and settlement of securities, resulting in high levels of transaction costs. As regards the region's legal systems, a number of economies still do not have well-developed securities laws. Furthermore, the legal and tax systems often tend to inadvertently inhibit bond market development; in some countries in the region, there exists a tax bias against bonds. Taxes such as withholding taxes, turnover taxes and stamp duties that are often imposed on bonds (but not on equities or bank deposits) can impede trade and result in segmented markets and reduced liquidity. Not surprisingly, such a tax bias is much disliked by institutional investors, and has impeded bond market development.

Accounting and Disclosure Standards

Until recently, many Asian economies have neglected the role of accounting as well as the role of accountants and auditors. The absence of high quality and comparable accounting standards on the financial position of businesses can inhibit investor interest in capital markets by increasing risk and uncertainty.

In recognition of this, a number of economies in the region have, in recent years, taken steps to enhance accounting standards and to reinforce the role of external auditors.

The disclosure of high-quality business information, provided in a timely manner, on the financial position of businesses is also critical to the efficient functioning of the financial system. Better business information enables potential investors to assess returns to capital as well as the associated risks. At the same time, it creates incentives for firms to improve their financial performance through such means as better governance. Better information also helps reduce transaction costs. Moreover, comparability of financial information on firms can play an important role in promoting greater cross-border capital flows. Not only would this spur greater cross-border investments and enable capital to flow across economies in search of highest returns, it would also assist capital-scarce economies in the region to tap the markets of capital-surplus economies, thereby alleviating bottlenecks in capital availability faced by some developing economies.

A number of economies in the region have made efforts to improve disclosure standards; toward the mid-1980s, the Republic of Korea, Malaysia, Singapore, Taipei,China, and Thailand made efforts to strengthen disclosure, and other economies in the region are making efforts to follow suit.

Credit Rating

A related concern is the need to develop credit rating agencies. While most economies have domestic credit rating agencies, these are not always entirely effective, credible and independent, and cannot therefore offer investors the assurance that risks are properly assessed. Indeed, effective and credible credit rating agencies are a key ingredient of domestic capital market development, particularly because of the assurance they offer investors, both foreign and domestic, that risks can be properly assessed. Not only do they help increase confidence in the market; they are also critical to minimizing transaction costs and ensuring market efficiency.

In recent years, several countries in the region have established credit rating agencies to boost their bond markets and ensure investor protection. For example, PRC, the Republic of Korea, and India now have several rating agencies in operation. The Indonesian agency (PEFINDO) was established only in November 1994 and its role is still evolving. Malaysia's RAM is now well-established and has been successful. Thailand's TRIS is relatively new, but has done well in stabilizing its presence in the market. However, some domestic rating agencies, for example, the Republic of Korea's KIS and the Philippines' CIBI, have been relatively less effective despite being in operation for more than a decade.

Development of the region's rating industry is constrained by several factors. First, a number of countries tend to impose guarantee requirements on bond issues, which act as an impediment to the development of the rating industry, by encouraging investors to rely on guarantees rather than on measuring and managing credit risks. Recently, efforts are being made to eliminate such requirements. The Republic of Korea, for example, has only recently eliminated this requirement.

Second, the absence of uniform accounting principles (that are fully in line with international accounting standards) and proper disclosure requirements pose a serious threat to the integrity and reliability of credit ratings.

Third, rating processes and analyses are not uniformly rigorous. The lack of highly trained professional analysts, the absence of uniform accounting and disclosure requirements, and the inability of an agency to function as an independent entity free from political influence all contribute to this. A particular issue is that agencies rate some domestic corporations above the country's sovereign risk limit.

Fourth, there exists a lack of transparency that causes difficulties for many non-insider investors in obtaining accurate, timely, and internationally comparable financial statements, reports on significant corporate events, and even accurate descriptions of outstanding securities. While there are a number of financial publishers who currently "collect" financial information, most of them have a problem in terms of serving a broad investment analysis market because of the composition of their traditional financial products and the difficulty of making their histories compatible.

Fifth, the asset allocation policies of institutional investors also influence the demand for ratings and, hence, the success of a credit rating agency. Institutional investors in most developing economies tend to be in the public sector, and tend to invest in government securities, thus failing to provide the necessary impetus for the rating industry.

Sixth, rating agencies are not generally profitable in the initial years of operation, owing mainly to high start-up and operating costs, lack of sufficient demand for rating, and a limited number of debt issues. Among the domestic rating agencies in the region, only RAM has so far been profitable, while CIBI posted its first year of profits in 1994 after being in existence for more than a decade.

Governments can play an important role in fostering the development of rating agencies. The first step in this regard would be to act decisively to remove remaining impediments such as guarantee requirements on bond issues. Second, governments could help stipulate uniform accounting and disclosure requirements for business information. A third measure would be to establish prudential regulations designed to encourage the use of ratings. Issuers must be convinced that obtaining a rating will provide access to a wider investor base for their securities and help reduce the cost of issuing debt. The United States has prudential regulations governing the quality of investments of such institutions as banks, insurance companies, and savings and loan associations. These regulations have provided incentives for issuers to be rated and contributed to the success of rating agencies in that country.

The domestic rating agencies, in turn, must make efforts to earn credibility by focusing more on the need to improve rating standards and improve market transparency and comparability of financial information across national borders. This, in turn, would involve focusing on the training and skills development of rating analysts and making concerted efforts in moving toward uniform accounting and disclosure requirements, and transparency. It would also involve ensuring that adequate software is developed/acquired so as to capture a variety of financial statements and to allow the broadest and most flexible distribution of the resulting work product.

In addition, a well-developed institutional investor (pension funds, mutual funds, insurance companies) industry would have a strong positive impact on the use of bond ratings, given that investors in bond markets tend to be predominantly institutional.

As the region's capital markets become more integrated with the further liberalization of capital flows, issuers will increasingly tap different markets in the region in search of low-cost capital, and investors will expand their universe of investment opportunities to maximize the return on their investments, regardless of where the issuers are based. In such a scenario, rating agencies face an additional challenge of rating issuers domiciled in other economies, and also the impact of sovereign risk on their ratings.

Clearing and Settlement Systems

Effective trading in the secondary market, particularly bond markets, depends on reliable and expeditious clearing, settlement, and payments systems. In essence, clearing and settlement[8] systems are essential for all transactions that involve delivery of payment at a later time. In the absence of well-developed clearing, settlement, and payment systems, traders run a variety of risks including counterparty risk, fraud, and multiple trades of the same security. Well-functioning clearing and settlement systems can guard against such risks.

A number of economies in the region suffer from an absence of modern and well-developed clearing and settlement systems. Typical elements of modern and efficient clearing and settlement

---

[8] Clearing essentially entails finding out if payment orders are backed up with available funds. The value of clearinghouses is accentuated in markets engaged in international transactions. A settlement system, meanwhile, involves the transfer of funds signifying completion of the transaction. In developed capital markets, securities are immobilized in a central depository for safekeeping. Transfer of securities is then accomplished using an electronic book entry system.

systems include a central depository for securities, which operates on a book-entry principle; "delivery versus payment" schemes (i.e., no buyer can take delivery before making payment, and no seller should receive the sales proceeds before transferring ownership) that help reduce risks; various mechanisms to guard against fraud; and mechanisms to create a clear segregation of customer accounts from those of dealers. In recent years, some economies have made efforts to establish modern clearing and settlement systems. Malaysia and Thailand are well-advanced in this area. Probably the most advanced and all-inclusive system is the Central Moneymarket Unit System (CMU) of Hong Kong.

Benchmarks

Benchmarks play a crucial role in the efficient functioning of both primary and secondary bond markets. They can be used to gauge the prevailing interest rate structure, market expectations on future interest rate movements, and inflation (and the associated risk premiums). Investors in fixed income securities are exposed to a variety of potential risks—for example, business risk, interest rate risk, market stability risk, purchasing power risk, and issue-specific risks—depending on the local market climate. Given the risks involved, the availability of market-based benchmarks is essential for the appropriate pricing of these securities. In industrial countries such as the US, prices of fixed income securities are based on US treasury securities, which are almost risk-free. A margin to cover credit risks and other specific risks is added to the prevailing yield on benchmark securities. Availability of a market-based benchmark also facilitates the development of other risk management instruments such as futures and options.

The defining characteristics of benchmark securities is their liquidity, which is often associated with regular and large issues. For benchmarks to be useful, the size of issuance should be large and cover the entire maturity spectrum to create a yield curve. Government bonds usually form the benchmark yield curve since they carry virtually no default risk. In the interest of attracting long-term capital, the benchmark yield curve must extend over the medium to long term.

In Asian economies, however, the development of risk-free yield curves has been somewhat limited. The main reason for this lack of market-based government security benchmarks has been the fact that many of these economies (except the PRC and the Philippines) have not been active issuers of bonds in view of their fiscal surpluses. Since most bonds are held to maturity by the contractual savings sector and financial institutions, secondary markets have been slow to develop. Another impediment to establishing benchmark yield curves has been the short maturity of bond issues. In addition, interest rate controls also hamper efforts to establish benchmarks.

In recent years, many economies in the region have made efforts to develop benchmark securities. The most successful story in recent years is that of Hong Kong. Owing to its healthy fiscal position, it had virtually no government bond market in the early 1990s. In 1990, the Government of Hong Kong introduced the Exchange Fund Bills and Notes Program to provide a tool for monetary management. In 1994, the Monetary Authority launched the five-year notes followed by a seven-year issue in 1995. Recently, it issued a ten-year government note. The gradual lengthening of the maturity of Exchange Fund Bills and Notes provided the benchmark for the issuance of debt instruments of longer maturities. Needless to say, the issue has been accompanied by developments in the clearing and settlement systems. The government established a cost-effective computerized book-entry clearing system, which considerably reduced settlement risk and facilitated secondary market trading not just of Exchange Bills and Notes, but also of other Hong Kong debt instruments.

CONCLUSION

This chapter has attempted to provide an overview of the financial reform efforts of Asian economies. As is evident from the discussion above, economies throughout Asia have, over the last decade, undertaken steps to reform their financial sectors— both the banking system and capital markets—by deregulating domestic financial markets and opening up these markets to greater private sector competition, both domestic and foreign. While specific reform measures have no doubt varied across economies, there exists a broad commonality in the overall objectives of reform—namely, to create competitive and efficient financial sectors that are equipped to meet the region's growing resource needs. The degrees of success achieved with the reform efforts have, of course, varied, with the East and Southeast Asian economies having clearly emerged as the leaders. But in economies throughout Asia, much still remains to be done in creating more resilient financial regimes. Creating a resilient banking system requires an acceleration of efforts directed at introducing greater diversification and competition, improved banking practices, and enhanced prudential oversight. The task of banking reforms is particularly urgent for the region's transition economies, and also for other economies throughout the region. Furthermore, as Asia's emerging market economies work toward mobilizing the capital required to finance the next stage of growth, and particularly toward mobilizing the much-needed long-term capital for financing infrastructure investment, the role of efficient capital markets, particularly bond markets, has gained center stage. While some economies in the region have initiated reforms to deepen capital markets, for most economies, the tasks ahead are significant.

The subsequent chapters of this volume identify and elaborate on the main challenges and policy options with regard to financial reform confronting the region and, in doing so, focus on the main themes of the seminar. While Chapter Two examines the broad policy challenges with financial reform facing economies in the region, Chapters Three, Four, and Five focus on the specific cases of PRC, Indonesia, and New Zealand, respectively. A set of presumptive indicators, or early warning signals, that should prove helpful in recognizing potential financial crises in emerging market economies is presented in Chapter Six. Chapter Seven contains a summary of discussions, including the comments of the three discussants, responses from the panelists, and questions from the floor. Finally, Chapter Eight presents the Chairman's summing-up.

REFERENCES

Amsden, A. 1989. *Asia's Next Giant: South Korea and Late Industrialization*. New York: Oxford University Press.

Andersen, Arthur. 1993. *Asia/Pacific Capital Markets: A Vision of Change*. UK: EIU.

Asian Development Bank. 1995 and 1996. "The Financial Sector and Asian Development: Historical Experiences and Prospects." *Asian Development Outlook 1995-1996*. Hong Kong: Oxford University Press.

Bank for International Settlements. 1996. 66th Annual Report.

Carroll, C., David N. Wiel, and Lawrence H. Summers. 1993. "Saving and Growth." Paper presented at the Bradley Policy Research Center's Carnegie-Rochester Public Policy Conference, Rochester, N.Y.

Dornbusch, R. 1984. "External Debt, Budget Deficits and Disequilibrium Exchange Rates." NBER Working Paper No. 4. Cambridge: National Bureau of Economic Research.

Hossain, A., and A. Chowdhury. 1996. *Monetary and Financial Policies in Developing Countries: Growth and Stabilization*. London: Routledge Studies in Development Economics.

International Monetary Fund. *International Financial Statistics*. (various issues). Washington, D.C.

Ito, Takatoshi, and David Folkerts-Landau. 1996. "International Capital Markets Developments, Prospects and Key Policy Issues." *World Economic and Financial Surveys*. Washington, D.C.: International Monetary Fund, September.

Khatkhate, D. R. 1972. "Analytical Basis of the Working of Monetary Policy in Less Developed Countries." IMF *Staff Papers*, vol. 19, no. 3.

Kim, Jong Il, and Lawrence Lau. 1994. "The Sources of Economic Growth of the East Asian Newly Industrialized Countries." *Journal of the Japanese and International Economies*, vol. 8.

King, R.G., and R. Levine. 1993a. "Finance, Entrepreneurship and Growth: Theory and Evidence." *Journal of Monetary Economics*, vol. 32, December.

King, R.G., and R. Levine. 1993b. "Financial Intermediation and Economic Development." In *Capital Markets and Financial Intermediation*, edited by C. Mayer and X. Vives. Cambridge: Cambridge University Press.

Kit Tam, On. 1995. *Financial Reform in China*. Routledge Studies in the Growth Economies of Asia. London: Routledge

Krugman, Paul. 1994. "The Myth of Asia's Miracle." *Foreign Affairs*, vol. 73, November-December.

McKinnon, Ronald I. 1991. *The Order of Economic Liberalization: Financial Control on the Transition to a Market Economy*. Baltimore: Johns Hopkins University Press.

McKinnon, Ronald I. 1989. "Financial Liberalization and Economic Development: A Reassessment of Interest Rate Policies in Asia and Latin America." *Oxford Review of Economic Policy*, vol. 5, no.4.

McKinnon, Ronald I. 1973. *Money and Capital in Economic Development*. Washington, D.C.: Brookings Institution.

Murray, Bruce, and Priya Basu. 1995. "Financial Reforms in the People's Republic of China: An Agenda for the Future." *Asian Development Bank Review*. Manila: Asian Development Bank, July-August.

Sarel, Michael. 1996. "Growth and Productivity in ASEAN Economies." Presented at an IMF Conference in Jakarta.

Shaw, E. 1973. *Financial Deepening in Economic Development*. New York: Oxford University Press.

Stiglitz, Joseph E. 1994. "The Role of the State in Financial Markets." Proceedings of the World Bank Annual Conference on Development Economics 1993, Supplement to *World Bank Economic Review* and *World Bank Research Observer*.

Stiglitz, Joseph E., and Marilou Uy. 1996. "Financial Markets, Public Policy and the East Asian Miracle." *The World Bank Research Observer*, vol. 11, no. 2.

Thirlwall, A.P. 1989. *Growth and Development with Special Reference to Developing Countries*. London: Macmillan.

Wade, R. 1988. "The Role of Government in Overcoming Market Failure: Taiwan, Republic of Korea and Japan." In *Achieving Industrialization in Asia*, edited by H. Hughes. Cambridge: Cambridge University Press.

World Bank. 1989. *World Development Report*. Washington, D.C.: World Bank.

Young, Alwyn. 1992. "Tale of Two Cities: Factor Accumulation and Technical Change in Hong Kong and Singapore." *National Bureau of Economic Research Economics Annual*.

CHAPTER TWO

TOWARD RESILIENT
FINANCIAL SYSTEMS

PAUL M. DICKIE

For most Asian countries, progress toward a resilient financial system is still incomplete. Although countries vary in their stage of progress toward that objective, all Asian countries have given market forces and the private sector a greater role in financial sector development. In conjunction with these increasingly market-based financial systems, Asian countries have also instituted more responsive policy regimes, placing increased reliance on indirect policy instruments to guide market outcomes. Nevertheless, much still needs to be done in most countries to achieve truly resilient financial systems, particularly as the global financial system itself is also in transition.

Five broad themes are explored in this chapter that are determining the progress toward resilient financial systems. These are also explored in more detail in subsequent chapters in the context of individual country experiences. The first theme relates to the nature and extent of government intervention in banking sectors. Most governments in the region have directly intervened in the financial sectors to a greater or lesser degree. Since the late 1970s, most governments in the region have begun to introduce more market forces in order to improve the allocation and mobilization of domestic resources. However, the varying conditions prior to reform have to some extent determined how transitions in particular countries have taken place, and the legacy of the old systems has for some countries impeded the progress of reforms. Transitions here have been broadly categorized into two groups: the transitional or the previous command economies and the inward-looking economies.

The second theme considers the disintermediation of commercial banking, which will occur as market forces are given more latitude and financial systems are reformed. Capital markets tend to be more cost effective, particularly in financing long-term infrastructure and business investments. Relative to banking, the growth of capital markets can be expected to accelerate rapidly with the economic development and market openings now underway in Asia.

The third theme looks at issues concerning the opening up of capital accounts in Asian countries to benefit from foreign capital and direct investments in particular, and associated issues of exchange rate management.

The fourth theme looks at the problems that are faced with the sequencing of financial sector reforms, given the need to accommodate more open capital flows. While the optimal order would liberalize interest rates and the domestic banking sector prior to opening the capital account, actual experience in Asia demonstrates that it is possible to violate this order of reform with very responsive and adaptable policy adjustments.

The fifth and final theme considers the urgent need for governments to improve their prudential regulations and looks at the regulatory challenge and supervision needs of Asian countries in creating resilient financial systems, particularly those where heavy state-directed banking systems and state-owned enterprises have left a legacy of bad debts.

In most of the economies of Asia, financial sectors are dominated by commercial banks, with over 75 percent of the financial assets in most emerging Asian countries controlled by the banking sector. In part, this reflects the region's high domestic savings rates, which have given banks an easy and captive source of funds. However, the high proportion of banking assets in the financial system, compared with the industrial countries, also demonstrates that Asia is at an early stage of financial sector development. Commercial banks not only dominate the financial sectors in Asian countries, but they are also very profitable, as demonstrated by economies such as Hong Kong, Malaysia, Republic of Singapore, and Kingdom of Thailand. In contrast, banking in many developed countries, such as the United States, is far less profitable and competition has forced many banks to merge under great stress and strain.

GOVERNMENT INTERVENTION

Most Asian governments have, in the past, directly intervened in their financial systems, albeit in varying degrees. They have created financial institutions, helped create financial markets, regulated these institutions and markets, controlled interest rates, and intervened directly to control money supply. They have also intervened in their banking sectors, whether by owning banks directly or by directed lending decisions, or both. These practices have fostered inefficiencies, most particularly in South Asia and in the transition economies of Asia. However, as governments have increasingly recognized the need for markets to allocate credit, financial sectors in Asia are being transformed.

There are two kinds of transitions that can be used as illustrations of the experiences in financial sectors in Asia. One type of transition, which has also taken place elsewhere in the developing world, is from an inward-looking to outward-looking development model. An inward-looking model characterized financial sectors in the 1960s and 1970s and was particularly adopted in South Asia, and also in other countries, such as the Republic of Indonesia. Reasonably high levels of protection were used to build up domestic industry and corresponding with those state-owned enterprises (SOEs), state-owned banks were developed. As Asia moved to a more outward-looking model in the late 1970s and early 1980s, opening up the economy to the outside world required not only reform of SOEs but also reform of financial sectors. These reform processes have not been easy and perhaps the most rapid adjustment from inward to outward-looking policies has taken place in Indonesia. The Indonesian experience of reform of the financial sector is discussed in detail in Chapter Four.

The second type of transition that has occurred in Asia has taken place in Asia's transitional or command economies. Under the command system, a single bank (also known as monobank), essentially acted as Treasurer; consequently, banking skills (other than those related to Treasury functions) were virtually nonexistent. In these economies, institutions typically did not have the capability of assessing when credits should be extended and when they should not. There was no use of asset/liability criteria to manage commercial banks, and no capability to assess a bank's riskiness. The three stages of financial sector reform in the People's Republic of China (PRC), which represents the most advanced country in transition, is presented in Chapter Three.

DISINTERMEDIATION OF COMMERCIAL BANKING

Financial reforms in Asia, ranging from the PRC's gradualist approach to Indonesia's rapid adjustment, have been impressive, as have the rapid economic growth and development in the more dynamic Asian economies. Over the next decade, it is expected that as capital markets in Asia's emerging market economies develop further, financial intermediation through equity and bond markets will increase in importance relative to intermediation through banks. On the one hand, as firms grow and mature, they are more likely to raise capital through equity and bond markets than to borrow from banks, as the latter entail higher costs. On the other hand, savers, too, may prefer to place their savings with mutual funds and other institutional investors that offer higher returns by investing people's cash directly in money markets, stocks and bonds. As the banking system is increasingly bypassed by both borrowers and savers and banking sector disintermediation accelerates, capital markets will come to dominate financial sector activities.[1] This is already beginning to happen in a number of Asian countries, particularly in the higher income East and Southeast Asian economies where capital markets are developing more rapidly (e.g., Hong Kong, Republic of Korea, and Singapore). India and Malaysia, where mutual funds are growing rapidly and becoming more popular as

---

[1] For example, in the United States the share of commercial banks in total financial assets has declined from over 60 percent in the early 1970s to under 30 percent in 1992. See Wheelock (1993). The decline of banking in the United States as well as in other countries, and the implications of these trends are discussed in Edwards and Mishkin (1995).

vehicles of household saving, are also experiencing financial disintermediation.

Financial disintermediation could also work towards strengthening banking systems in Asia, as capital markets help spread the risks previously concentrated in banks. For example, an increased reliance by property companies on equity and on increased use of mortgage-backed securitization should help reduce the exposure of banks to the real estate sector. In addition, well-developed debt markets extending into long maturities can help banks limit maturity mismatches in their balance sheets.

Moreover, the threat of disintermediation could prove to be the driving force in the redefinition and restructuring of banking functions.[2] Already, some countries in the region are moving more toward universal banking practices. In Malaysia and Singapore, and also in Thailand, big commercial banks now have investment banking and stockbroking arms that deal with issuing, underwriting, placing, and trading securities.

OPENING UP THE FOREIGN CAPITAL ACCOUNT AND EXCHANGE RATE MANAGEMENT

Foreign capital inflows into emerging Asian economies have increased rapidly in the 1990s, as a result of the liberalization and internationalization of financial systems, the rigorous macroeconomic policies (including high interest rates) pursued by them, and the continuing commitment of these countries to liberal financial markets. Investors have become increasingly attracted by higher yielding alternatives in Asian countries, both in terms of interest rates on short-term paper and bank deposits and on securities; in 1995 capital flows to Asian developing countries accounted for 50 percent of capital flows to all developing countries.[3] Net private capital inflows into developing Asian countries amounted to US$151 billion during 1990-1993, US$81.1 billion in 1994, and US$104.1 billion in 1995. Over half of these

---

[2] Assessing the efficiency of commercial banks is not a simple task and there are large variations in the various measures of efficiency; see Wheelock and Wilson (1995).

[3] Ito and Folkerts-Landau (1996).

inflows were in the form of foreign direct investment, which is the more stable form of foreign investment. However, a significant volume of inflows came in the form of short-term deposits; this reflects the marked fall in short-term interest rates in the major industrial countries (especially the United States and Japan). While the bulk of these inflows have been concentrated in a few East and Southeast Asian developing countries, recently, South Asian countries, such as India, Kingdom of Nepal, and Democratic Socialist Republic of Sri Lanka, have also experienced relatively large capital inflows. Capital inflows have helped facilitate growth and development in developing Asian countries.

Equally, an open capital account introduces high degrees of volatility which can result in financial crises. Mexico's financial crisis in 1995, and the recent bout of exchange rate troubles being faced by Southeast Asian countries, are testament to the problems that can result from international capital flows into, and out of, emerging economies ill-prepared to deal with them.

A number of economies in Southeast Asia have traditionally been committed to maintaining stable exchange rates, and have, in the past, done so by linking their currencies to the dollar with intervention in the foreign exchange markets to maintain the fixed rate. One of the problems is that an implicit exchange rate guarantee is being provided via the unchanged dollar link. As domestic monetary policy will often involve high real interest rates, local residents can borrow US dollars short term and relend with higher returns in local currency. This incentive to build up short-term external debt can be a major problem if exchange rate uncertainty emerges due to the economy moving away from a position of full competitiveness. Over the past two years, such developments have materialized in part because of the strong appreciation of the US dollar which rose against the Yen by more than 30 percent. As there was also a buildup in short-term external debt in Thailand due to the interest rate differential and the implicit exchange rate guarantee, the first speculative attacks emerged relative to the Thai baht. The Philippine peso, the Indonesian rupiah, and the Malaysian riggit came under pressure in turn. In each of these cases, and particularly in Thailand, the exchange rate corrections could have taken place earlier—by a smaller amount and in a less chaotic fashion, if a more flexible exchange rate policy had been in place. Other than in Indonesia, officials were reluctant to adopt flexible exchange rate policies partly because depreciation of the currency was seen as having unfavorable political costs (a point which will be discussed in greater detail in Chapter Six), and also because market volatility was seen to have economic costs. As such, there was a tendency to delay the needed adjustments.

There is no major problem with competitiveness in East Asia. While there has been a regional trend of declining export growth, this was also associated with an earlier inventory buildup in the electronics industry. Moreover, in the case of the Philippines, for example, exports were in fact up 23 percent in May 1997 from a year earlier, which hardly suggested that the currency was over-valued. The country's current account deficit (4.5 percent of GDP) was also much smaller than Thailand's (about 8 percent last year). Nevertheless, the Philippines runs a much bigger trade deficit, financed in large measure by remittances from the larger number of overseas Filipino workers. Fear that a weak currency might deter overseas Filipinos from sending their remittances home has been an important factor determining the government's reluctance, in the past, to allow peso depreciation. At the same time, there had been a buildup of short-term debts in Thailand and, to a much lesser extent, in some of the other economies in the region. Local financial institutions and companies that have borrowed dollars could face repayment difficulties with the depreciation of the local currency.

In the event, and despite resistance, Thailand, the Philippines, and Malaysia have all been forced to introduce or, in the case of Indonesia, to increase the flexibility of their links to the dollar. In each case, floating the currency has resulted in a depreciation during July 1997; the Thai baht fell by 26 percent, while the Philippine peso, the Indonesian rupiah, and the Malaysian riggit have suffered smaller depreciations in the 4–10 percent range.

Southeast Asian economies now face a difficult task. They will need to contain the inflation that will follow from devaluation as well as exploit their increased export competitiveness. They will also need to accept some increased degree of currency volatility. Hopefully, they will not try once again to keep their currencies within a narrow trading range, through intervention in the foreign exchange markets. Over the longer run, they will need to develop more resilient, market-based financial sectors that can assist in successfully managing capital flows to the benefit of these economies.

Opening up the capital account also presents possible problems with overborrowing for Asian countries. Capital inflows from foreign depositors who speculate on domestic currencies and place funds into, say, 3- or 6-month deposits, are not much different, in terms of the banking sector, from a 3- or 6-month loan. Both types of inflows are liabilities of the banking system that have to be managed, and, in that sense, the *"overborrowing phenomena"*, as defined by McKinnon,[4] is just as applicable in Asia as in Latin America, even though most Asian countries do not actively seek funds. The pressures of an open capital account complicate financial and fiscal reform. When the policy mix is not right, resulting capital flows, in both directions, constitute a policy scorecard that cannot be ignored, as evidenced in India where nonresident accounts have flowed in and out depending on perceptions regarding the exchange rate and markets.

SEQUENCING OF FINANCIAL SECTOR REFORMS

Macroeconomic stability is often blamed for the failures of financial liberalization in developing countries. However, the strategy of financial liberalization itself may add to macroeconomic instability and compound the problem. It is generally believed that any premature opening up of the capital account in the balance of payments during economic reform may generate macroeconomic instability and destabilizing capital flows. This conventional approach to sequencing, associated primarily with the works of McKinnon and Dornbusch,[5] calls for gradual and properly sequenced liberalization. The *"optimal"* order of economic liberalization, according to this approach, is one in which the strengthening and liberalization of interest rates and the domestic banking sector precedes trade and current account liberalization.

On the domestic side, it is argued that fiscal control should precede financial liberalization. Thus, before price controls can

---

[4] McKinnon (1996).

[5] Ibid; McKinnon (1993); McKinnon (1989); McKinnon (1973); Dornbusch (1984).

be phased out, and before capital markets can be opened up, the central government's finances must be balanced. In other words government spending must be limited, and a broad-based tax system, with low tax rates and capable of raising sufficient revenue to avoid inflation, should be in place. In the transition economies, where all or part of the means of production have tended to be government-owned, these assets cannot be safely privatized until a full-fledged internal revenue service is in place capable of collecting taxes from the private sector. In the meantime, government-owned enterprises should continue to provide revenue for the public treasury. Otherwise, rapid liberalization could lead to higher deficits in the public finances. In addition, any off-budget government subsidies should be included in the regular balanced budget or be phased out.

Second in the order of liberalization is the opening up of domestic capital markets. This is necessary for achieving positive real (inflation-adjusted) interest rates–both deposit rates and borrowing rates. However, this can only proceed satisfactorily once the price level is stabilized and fiscal deficits are eliminated. Also, the banking system should only be freed from high reserve requirements, and official guidance in setting interest rates on deposits and loans removed, once tight fiscal controls are in place. This is necessary so that governments no longer rely on the inflation tax or undue reserve taxes on depositors to generate revenues.

The pace of deregulation of banks and other financial institutions in liberalizing economies must be carefully geared to the government's success in achieving overall macroeconomic stability. Without price-level stability, unpredictable volatility in real interest rates or exchange rates makes unrestricted domestic borrowing and lending by deposit-taking banks too risky. Borrowing and lending must be regulated to ensure the safety of the payments mechanism. Because of the moral hazard associated with "private" monetary intermediaries, whose deposit base remains insured (implicitly or explicitly) by the government, the decentralization of the banking system through private ownership or control of the commercial banks should come near the end of the reform process.

Before opening up the international capital account on the balance of payments, the domestic capital market should be fully liberalized. This, in turn, depends on the stabilization of the domestic price level and the elimination of reserve taxes on domestic banks and other monetary intermediaries. So long as domestic banks are restricted and heavily taxed, it is destabilizing to the domestic banking sector to allow foreign banks or other foreign financial institutions to operate freely in domestic financial markets. It is also destabilizing to allow foreign currencies to circulate in parallel with a "soft" domestic currency. Only when domestic borrowing and lending take place freely at equilibrium rates of interest and the domestic rate of inflation is curbed so that ongoing depreciation in the exchange rate is unnecessary are the arbitrage conditions right for allowing free international capital mobility. Free foreign exchange convertibility on the capital account is usually the last stage in the optimal order of economic liberalization.

It is interesting to note that while there is general consensus that the foregoing sequence of reforms is appropriate, Indonesia undertook the reform of their financial sector in the 1980s under conditions of an open capital account which had been established in 1971. However, any misalignment in domestic policies during this deregulation phase gave rise to large-scale capital flows that necessitated rapid policy adjustments. While it may be possible to violate the reform sequencing, as Indonesia demonstrated, the optimum sequencing of reforms provides a much more manageable and prudent approach.

THE REGULATORY CHALLENGE

Rapid economic reform in Asia has brought increasingly deregulated and diversified banking and financial sectors in recent years, with demands for a broader range of financial products and services. Doors are being opened to foreign banks and other financial institutions, even in countries that had hitherto blocked such competition. In this context, deregulation of financial systems and reducing government ownership and leaving markets to allocate scarce resources and to impose market discipline, has changed the regulatory challenge and led to a need for banking regulation and supervision to take on an altogether new dimension. On the one hand, there is an urgent need to enhance the system of prudential oversight to cope with the increased risks that are associated with greater liberalization. On the other hand, there is also a need to ensure that institutions, such as banks, assume greater responsibility for these increased risks.

Commercial banks still face significant problems in countries throughout developing Asia, particularly in the transition economies and in South Asia, and also in other Asian economies. Many banks today are characterized by bad debts to nonperforming SOEs–an outcome of directed lending policies pursued in the past. As countries liberalize and open up their banking sectors, tackling problems related to the bad debts of domestic banks has become even more urgent, as has the need for governments to improve prudential regulations and supervision. In addition, it is seen that banking and enterprise reforms must be mutually reinforcing to ensure that enterprises operate on a competitive, profit-oriented basis. This will enable the banking sector to impose financial discipline on a group of relatively sound borrowers. Minimum capital adequacy requirements are a primary tool of effective prudential regulation of banking systems as banks' capital serves as a protection for depositors. The most prominent capital/asset rule is the 8 percent BIS capital adequacy ratio, and many emerging Asian market economies have moved slowly toward meeting this regulation. Other significant prudential rules that have also been strengthened in many countries include limits on the entry of new institutions, limitations on loans to insiders and on the size of loans that could be extended to any single borrower, and more rigorous auditing and accounting standards.

The high-income economies of the Republic of Korea, Hong Kong, Singapore, and Taipei,China were among the earliest in the region to endorse the BIS adequacy standard of 8 percent capital-to-asset risk-weighted ratios; capital adequacy ratios in Hong Kong and Singapore exceed 15 percent. For the most part, other East and Southeast Asian countries (Indonesia, Malaysia, Philippines, and Thailand) have also met, or are moving toward meeting the 8 percent standard. Other countries have yet to meet or even adopt the BIS standard. However, the BIS 8 percent standard was meant to be only a minimum for industrial countries, and supervisors or banks in riskier environments of emerging markets might, in fact, need to impose higher ratios to achieve a proper safeguard.[6] This is particularly so in Asian countries where measures of capital are not so accurate because of poor accounting practices, or where incomplete recognition of nonperforming assets has often undermined the effectiveness of the capital adequacy ratio. A higher capital adequacy would also be necessary in countries such as the PRC, India and Indonesia, where nonperforming loans are mainly concentrated in the state sector.

Bad debts in Asian banks have also occurred because of the concentration on loans for real estate or other long-term investment in narrowly concentrated areas; the latter is particularly a problem in economies where production (especially exports) is narrowly concentrated in only a few commodities and offers banks limited scope for diversification. Lending to connected enterprises in a number of Asian countries has made objective risk assessment difficult. Rules on maximum exposure limits to a single borrower may also have been set too high in the past. Asian countries vary in this regard, with the range of limits varying from 10 percent to 30 percent. Excessive maturity and currency mismatches between assets and liabilities are another problem for some countries. In addition, foreign currency lending to domestic borrowers has not been monitored and has led to banks in some countries facing severe problems. These weaknesses have led to the insolvency of two private sector banks in Indonesia, which have been dealt with in an effective manner by the Indonesian Government. A number of private banks also failed in the Philippines and Thailand as a result of nonperforming loans. Some Korean banks have experienced similar difficulties, and were saved only by large-scale intervention by the government.

As part of their regulatory system, several central banks in Asia (notably in India, Indonesia, Malaysia, and Thailand) have resorted to moral suasion to moderate credit expansion. Moral

---

[6] The Bank for International Settlements is coordinating a group of central banks and regulators, including emerging market economies, on a new set of bank supervisory guidelines that will constitute best practices in the area of minimum capital requirements, internal bank controls, monitoring of corporate lending practices, the need for external editors and full disclosure practices. These guidelines are expected to be approved by governments and issued by September 1997. For a general review of the issues, see International Monetary Fund (1996). For a review of the appropriate role of the capital requirements, see Estrella (1995).

suasion has also been applied to limit the rapid expansion of lending for investment in certain areas, such as in property or equities. Regular monthly meetings with the banking sector have been an important measure in some countries to encourage moral suasion. In some countries, banks are asked to submit their credit plans so that the central bank can assess the consequences on both macroeconomic stability and their financial condition. These measures are often used in countries where liberalization has not progressed enough to ensure sound banking operations.

The Indonesian experience of the late 1980s provides a good example of the perils of banking deregulation in the absence of a well-developed regulatory regime. Indonesia liberalized its banking sector in the 1980s, with the pace of reforms accelerating under the *PAKTO* program initiated in 1988. A plethora of new private banks were allowed entry, and access to credit became much easier, boosting economic growth. But these benefits did not come without a price. The existing regulatory and legal framework was unable to cope with the newly diversified and highly competitive banking system and there were not enough supervisors and auditors. The rapid expansion of the banking sector exposed banks to such risks as diluted standards of credit evaluation and portfolio supervision, poor loan recovery, deterioration in portfolio quality, and large losses. The impact of the *PAKTO* reforms on the banking sector thus highlighted the inadequacies of the then existing regulatory and legal framework to cope with the requirements of a rapidly growing financial system. The authorities were faced with the immediate task of reestablishing sufficient confidence to allow the financial sector to sustain its growth path, and tough steps had to be taken in respect of financial sector legislation, regulation and supervision. Measures to consolidate the gains and minimize the hazards generated by the newly liberalized banking and financial environment were embodied in the government's *PAKFEB* Program, launched in February 1991.

While the importance of maintaining financial stability is now widely recognized, there is no unique recipe for the effective regulation and supervision of the banking sector. As mentioned above, in some countries, fears of systemic risk in banking have led to calls for more rules and regulations and for the authorities to assume an ever greater supervisory responsibility. However, excessive regulation and supervision by the authorities can also lead to problems related to moral hazard, which calls into question traditional approaches to banking regulation and supervision. Moral hazard in banking systems increases as the authorities of countries assume more responsibility for risk through supervision and other protective schemes such as deposit insurance. These reduce the incentive for banks to pay attention to their own risk management and increase the risk that the taxpayer will have to bear the cost of bailing out failed banks. The Savings and Loan debacle in the United States and, more recently, a series of banking crises in Japan amply demonstrate problems of moral hazard in banking supervision.

Indeed, the problem of moral hazard creates a real dilemma for governments: without regulatory measures and a proper safety net for depositors/investors, financial and capital market failures could devastate an economy. However, with the safety nets, the number of financial and capital market institutions taking risks could rise. The challenge then is to achieve the optimal level and type of regulation.

To a large extent, the type of regulatory model adopted should depend on the stage of development of an economy; the stage of development of the supporting institutional infrastructure, including the legal system and the ability to enforce laws; the prevailing accounting and auditing systems and standards; the sophistication of savers, investors, borrowers, and issuers; and disclosure standards. At an early stage of economic development, proactive regulatory regimes may facilitate market development. In the long run, however, an effective regulatory system is one that is designed to regulate rather than control or manage the market and market participants. Disclosure standards are particularly important to move from traditional regulatory approaches to market-based approaches.

Furthermore, as economies move to disclosure-based regulatory systems that rely on market discipline, accounting, legal and analytical skills will need to be upgraded.[7] With the rapid increase in financial and capital market activity experienced in recent years both domestically and across borders, and with

---

[7] For a discussion of the role of financial regulation, economic cycle impacts and bad debt performance in Asia, see Huh and Kim (1994).

greater competition and diversification in financial and capital markets, the task of regulators is becoming ever more complex. Some central bankers in the region are beginning to admit that the traditional approach to banking regulation and supervision, where authorities assume all responsibilities, is ineffective and needs to be rethought. Notable in this context is New Zealand's pioneering approach to market-based regulation of the banking sector, which is discussed in greater detail in Chapter Five.[8]

CONCLUSION

The magnitude of the challenges faced by policy makers and financial sector practitioners in reforming Asia's financial sectors needs to be kept in mind. Asia has enormous needs for long-term capital and that means more open capital accounts to attract foreign direct investment, as well as rapid development of domestic capital markets. It is perhaps surprising that Asia has made more progress on attracting long-term capital than it has on developing domestic capital markets. This is especially true since the use of long-term debt capital from abroad leads to currency mismatch in most domestic applications such as infrastructure where the revenues are in local currency. To access both sources of long-term capital, there needs to be an appropriate sequencing of reforms to engender increased reliance on market forces, institutional support, as well as on increased use of indirect policy instruments to guide market outcomes. Such approaches will correspondingly lead to increasingly resilient financial systems. How such systems can best be evolved in individual countries is elaborated in Chapters Three to Six while the views of panelists on these topics are summarized in Chapter Seven.

---

[8] Another set of reform proposals has been issued in the United States by the Bank Administration Institute (see McKinsey and Company [1996]). The proposals are intended to ensure that regulation does not hinder banks from performing their function and includes proposals to ensure a level playing field, functionally focused as opposed to institutionally focused regulations and value-added supervision.

REFERENCES

Dornbusch, R. 1984. "External Debt, Budget Deficits and Disequilibrium Exchange Rates." NBER Working Paper No. 4. Cambridge: National Bureau of Economic Research.

Edwards, Franklin R., and Frederic S. Mishkin. 1995. "The Decline of Traditional Banking: Implications for Financial Stability and Regulatory Policy." *Economic Policy Review*, Federal Reserve Bank of New York, vol. 1, no. 2.

Estrella, Arturo. 1995. "A Prolegomenon to Future Capital Requirements." *Economic Policy Review*, Federal Reserve Bank of New York, vol. 1, no. 2.

Huh, Chon, and Sun Bae Kim. 1994. "Financial Regulation and Banking Sector Performance: A Comparison of Bad Loan Problems in Japan and Korea." *EconomicReview*, Federal Reserve Bank of San Francisco, no. 2.

International Monetary Fund. 1996. "Managing Risks to the International Banking System." *Financial Development*, vol. 33, no. 4.

Ito, Takatoshi, and David Folkerts-Landau. 1996. "International Capital Markets Developments, Prospects and Key Policy Issues," *Word Economic and Financial Surveys*. Washington, D.C.: International Monetary Fund.

McKinnon, Ronald I. 1996. *Credible Liberalizations and International Capital Flows: the "Overborrowing Syndrome."* Report submitted to the Asian Development Bank.

McKinnon Ronald I. 1993. *The Order of Economic Liberalization: Financial Control in the Transition to a Market Economy.* 2nd edition. Baltimore: Johns Hopkins University Press.

McKinnon Ronald I. 1989. "Financial Liberalization and Economic Development: A Reassessment of Interest Rate Policies in Asia and Latin America. *Oxford Review of Economic Policy*, vol. 5, no. 4.

McKinnon Ronald I. 1973. *Money and Capital in Economic Development.* Washington, D.C.: Brookings Institution.

McKinsey and Company. 1996. *Building Better Banks: The Case for Performance-based Regulation.* Chicago: Bank Administration Institute.

Wheelock, David C. 1993. "Is the Banking Industry in Decline? Recent Trends and Future Prospects from a Historical Perspective." *Review*, Federal Reserve Bank of Saint Louis, vol. 75, no. 5.

Wheelock, David, C., and Paul W. Wilson. 1995. "Evaluating the Efficiency of Commercial Banks: Does Our View of What Banks Do Matter?" *Review*, Federal Reserve Bank of Saint Louis, vol. 77, no. 4

CHAPTER THREE

THE THREE STAGES OF FINANCIAL SECTOR REFORM IN THE PEOPLE'S REPUBLIC OF CHINA

LI RUOGU

The PRC embarked on a process of financial reform in 1979. Financial reforms over the last 17 years have resulted in significant changes in the PRC's financial system, and have also contributed greatly to the country's economic growth. Roughly speaking, these financial reforms have been undertaken in three stages. The first, from 1979 to 1984, was characterized by the beginning of financial reform and the establishment of a Central Bank; the second stage, from 1985 to 1994, involved the diversification of the financial system and the development of the financial institutions; and the third stage, from 1995 onward, marks a consolidation of the reforms undertaken so far, pointing to the tasks and challenges ahead.

STAGE 1 - BEGINNING OF FINANCIAL REFORM AND ESTABLISHMENT OF A CENTRAL BANK

The PRC started its financial sector reform in 1979. For the 30 years from 1949 to 1979 the People's Bank of China (PBC), which functioned both as a commercial bank and a central bank, was the only bank in China. With the beginning of the economic reforms, it became clear that the PBC could not perform these dual tasks, so the idea of a two-tier banking system was proposed and implemented. First, the Agriculture Bank was established and then the Bank of China. They were followed by the People's Construction Bank of China and the Industrial and Commercial Bank of China.

In September 1983, the State Council issued a decree that the PBC would function solely as a central bank. Until that time, although a two-tier banking system had been set up, the PRC's financial system retained many of the features of a centrally planned economy. For example, although four banks had been operating since 1979, each operated in its own field and scope of business as a monopolist, with virtually no competition. However, despite the incomplete nature of the structural change that had taken place between 1979 and 1983, this period represented the first step toward a modern banking system and, more importantly, it represented a complete break from the ideas and practice of banking that had prevailed over the 30-year period from 1949 to 1979.

STAGE 2 - DEVELOPMENT OF FINANCIAL INSTITUTIONS

In the 17 years since 1979, the PRC economy has achieved remarkable progress with an average annual growth rate of 9 percent. This might not seem to be a very impressive achievement, since there were also several economies in the world that had enjoyed similar success. However, what makes the PRC's economic development exceptional is that it has been achieved by a country with a vast territory, relatively limited arable land, and the world's largest population. Within a relatively short span of 17 years, hundreds of millions of people were relieved from poverty and at the same time employment opportunities were created, both at home and abroad as a result of the PRC becoming the world's 11th largest trading power. Instead of impeding world economic development and draining away scarce resources, like some other transition economies, the PRC's economic reform and development have contributed significantly to the growth of wealth in the world.

Rapid economic growth in the PRC has also generated a growing need for financial services. In response to this demand, the PRC's financial sector evolved rapidly during the period between 1985 to 1994, although obviously with some fluctuations.

First, many new domestic banks were established, and by 1994, some 13 commercial banks were in operation. These new banks include the Bank of Communications, Shenzhen Development Bank, Guangdong Development Bank, CITIC Industrial Bank, Everbright Bank of China, Pudong Development Bank, Huaxia Bank, Hainan Development Bank (1950), and Minsheng Bank of China. Further competition was introduced into the financial sector with the entry of foreign banks together with overlapping and competing areas of business of the state-owned specialized banks. Although competition remained limited, there was a marked improvement in financial efficiency.

Second, nonbank financial institutions flourished and expanded rapidly, rising in number from zero in 1985 to more than 700 institutions by 1994. These institutions provided a variety of services to the fast growing economy and to meet the increasing needs of commercial enterprises, and supplemented the insufficient services provided by state-owned specialized banks. In addition, the number of urban and rural credit cooperatives expanded rapidly to over 56,000. They made a significant contribution to economic growth by extending financial assistance to a large number of Township and Village Enterprises (TVEs) and to the non-state sector. Meanwhile, the low quality of personnel working in nonbanking financial institutions and the lack of both adequate human capacity and a supervisory and regulatory framework in the institutions led to a number of serious problems, such as illegal fund raising, operating without a license, and other gray area activities. This caused a large loss of funds due to cheating, counterfeiting of certificates, and other illegal activities.

To solve these problems, the Government launched two initiatives, one in 1988 and a second in 1994. The nonbank financial institutions were closely scrutinized and their number was halved from more than 700 to around 350. The scope of their business was redefined and standardized, and stricter supervision rules and practices were introduced. Although it was clear that a measure of order had been restored, it was still unrealistic to expect the financial sector to function perfectly. Continuous actions through improved supervision and regulatory methods are still needed to allow the financial system to function more efficiently.

Third, foreign banks were introduced into the PRC with the first representative office being established in Beijing in 1979. As of the end of 1995, there were about 137 foreign financial institutions or branches of foreign banks operating in 24 open cities in the PRC. The open cities started from four special zones and expanded into 24 new cities. Currently, these foreign financial institutions have a very limited range of business activity, but their participation in the Chinese financial markets has brought more competition, advanced banking technology and managerial skills, which have had a very profound impact on the financial sector in the PRC. This has been widely recognized and appreciated by customers in the country.

Fourth, financial markets are gradually emerging in the PRC after nearly 40 years of absence. The PRC has been moving from indirect to direct financing by issuing securities and establishing stock exchanges in Shanghai and Shenzhen. The money market was first established in 1985, but still remains predominantly an interbank market. Although it is still very primitive, this market will become the focal point for the liberalization of interest rates in the coming years. Since the mid-1980s, more than RMB400 billion have been mobilized to support economic development through the issuance of treasury bills, financial and industrial bonds, stocks and other forms of securities. These reforms are regarded as a crucial step toward establishing a modern financial market in the PRC as they have broadened the base of the country's financial assets and resources. The development of secondary markets can be seen through the rapid growth of the two stock exchanges. The Shanghai stock exchange, for example, after less than three years of operation, had reached an annual total turnover of RMB2 trillion by 1994. The PRC attaches importance to the continued development of a secondary market as it increases the liquidity, accessibility, and attractiveness of securities, which in turn results in an expanded and more efficient financial sector. This in turn strengthens the foundations on which a market economy can be built.

Fifth, the foreign exchange system has undergone fundamental reform with the abolition of a dual exchange rate system.

A foreign exchange market was established in Shanghai in 1994 and, in the first year of its operation, the total value of transactions was US$61.4 billion. Further the RMB has evolved from being a nonconvertible currency to being fully convertible for current account transactions.

Sixth, the financial legal system has also been reformed over the last ten years or so and quite a number of financial laws and regulations have been put into effect. The basis of a Chinese financial legal system has been established by the promulgation and effectivity of the People's Bank Law, the Commercial Bank Law, and the Negotiable Instruments Law.

Seventh, after years of hesitation, the state-owned specialized banks have finally embarked on the road to commercialization. To this end special banks were established in 1994 to take over policy-based subsidized lending mandated by the Government. This move provides a foundation for transition from a centrally planned banking system by allowing specialized banks to compete with other banks on equal and commercial terms, and establishes a basis for further financial opening and further transition from a centrally planned system. Needless to say, banking reform will not succeed or be complete without a fundamental restructuring of state enterprises.

Finally, the process of formulating and implementing monetary policy has been changed dramatically. Prior to 1979, and even during the initial years of economic reform, the PBC acted only as cashier and accountant to the Ministry of Finance. However, since then monetary policy has been evolving from a passive and direct mode to a more active mode with the greater use of a combination of direct and indirect policy instruments, and with an increasing emphasis on the role of monetary policy to sustain economic growth at a low inflation rate. It is expected that the role of PBC will evolve so as to encompass a wider responsibility on PBC's part for economic performance through the administration of monetary policy and financial regulation through open market operations (which PBC initiated in 1996), management of interest and exchange rates, and other indirect monetary tools in order to achieve the targets set by the Government.

Many other areas of financial reform that have also taken place in the PRC include banking supervision, collection and publication of data and statistics, financial education and personnel training, and experiments with urban and rural cooperative banks.

STAGE 3 - CHINESE FINANCIAL REFORM IN PERSPECTIVE: TASKS, CHALLENGES, AND EXPERIENCES

After 17 or so years of reform, the PRC's financial sector looks entirely different. It now plays an active, supportive and growing role in the economic development of the country. However, for the financial sector to fulfill its function properly, much more remains to be done.

First of all, the existing interest rate system needs to be liberalized and replaced by a market interest rate mechanism. However, before this goal can be achieved, state-owned enterprises (SOEs) must be restructured. This is one of the most difficult sectors, if not the most difficult, to tackle. On the one hand, reform of SOEs is necessary for the healthy functioning of the financial sector, while, on the other hand, reform leads to concerns about social stability and involves a change in the way of life and of thinking. Therefore, although interest rate reform is a financial issue, it depends on many other factors and a cautious and comprehensive approach is needed. The urgency and need to complete this reform as soon as possible are also well-recognized, and the delay in interest rate liberalization has been the cause of many malfunctions in the financial system as well as illegal financial activities, and distortions in economic behavior. However, given the nature and complexity of the issue, it would not be a good idea to try to complete this reform in an unrealistically short period of time. The PRC has experienced very successful economic development during a very difficult economic transition from a centrally planned to a market-based economy and it is important that a process take place that will build consensus on the importance of fundamental reform in the financial sector. Through consensus reform, a financial sector will be created that is deep, more profound, integrated, and complete even though the difficulties and sufferings may be considerable.

Second, commercialization of the banking system is one of the key tasks for the PRC in the coming years. Specialized banks need to separate further their previous policy-based loans from the newly extended commercial loans, and to continue to clear up their balance sheets in order to meet the prudential requirements of commercial banking. More banks will be established in the next few years, especially urban and rural cooperative banks (which will be among the first group to be established). The restructuring of former urban and rural credit cooperatives is a great challenge for the authorities, since it covers not only institutional change but also changes in managerial ideas, and behavioral changes. Foreign banks will be allowed to do local currency operations on an experimental basis. These measures will enhance market competitiveness in the financial sector, thus increasing efficiency and improving financial services. However, although it is easy to list the number of things to be done in the area of financial reform, fulfilling these will take both time and effort.

Third, the insurance system needs substantial reform, with asset insurance, life insurance, and reinsurance separated from each other. More commercial insurance companies need to be set up in order to break the monopoly enjoyed by the People's Insurance Company, which has been a dominant company in the insurance market in the PRC over several decades.

Fourth, the PRC's foreign exchange reserves have been growing rapidly and are currently at over US$100 billion. Although a country like the PRC needs relatively high foreign exchange reserves for protection from various political and economic uncertainties, deciding on the appropriate and sufficient level of reserves, and on how the reserves should be used and managed are among the key challenges facing the authorities. The RMB's convertibility is another issue to be addressed in the next few years.

Fifth, central bank reform should be deepened. The stop/go cycles of the past decade have been a problem for economic development in the PRC. To avoid these vicious stop/go cycles, effective central macro control mechanisms must be established. PBC has to develop and install a system based on a market-oriented financial sector and also has to gain experience in macro management. Both will take time. Developing effective macroeconomic management and supporting sustainable high growth rates will be the greatest challenge facing the central bank over the next two to three decades.

Supervision and the regulation of financial activities will be another major role for the central bank to play. Rapid globalization in financial markets and the fast development of financial technology and instruments put increasing pressure on central banks to maintain stable and sound financial markets. A strong and sophisticated banking supervision and regulatory system needs to be in place with skilled staff in order to prevent possible crises in financial markets, given the increasingly complicated financial transactions and frequent financial scandals which are surfacing in the PRC. To fulfill this goal, international cooperation among central banks needs to be strengthened.

How to catch up with technological development and use it to provide and improve financial service will be another major task ahead for PBC. Modern technology has developed quickly, and has changed the idea and practice of today's banking. In this context, a major task for PBC is to establish an efficient, trouble-free, and secure national payments system.

Lastly, another great challenge to the central bank is to develop a sophisticated and advanced financial, and capital markets, in order to mobilize sufficient funds needed for the PRC's economic development.

To conclude, the last 17 years of financial reform in the PRC have brought many advantages. First, economic development together with financial reform has made people rich, with per capita financial assets increasing from RMB40 to RMB3,000 since 1979. Total household deposits jumped from less than RMB40 billion in 1978 to RMB3,000 billion (or RMB3 trillion) in 1995, a 62.5 time increase. This does not include several hundred million RMB securities issued in the last ten years or so. Second, the investment rate has grown by 30 to 40 percent per year during the last 17 years, and accumulated fixed assets in investments in the last five years amounted to more than RMB6.1 trillion. These high growth rates in financial and real assets have been the main resources for maintaining an annual average growth rate of 9 percent for about two decades. Third, positive real interest rates have contributed greatly to sustaining the high savings rate. The Government has taken every measure available to keep the interest rate positive, and although this is not a cost-free approach, it has been proven to be a successful one, judging by the country's economic development.

It is important that the benefits of reform reach the people; otherwise, the reform efforts will likely fail to generate sufficient political and economic strength to continue.

A dual system, such as what the PRC has at present, may not be a bad practice. When an old system moves to a new one, it is impossible to establish overnight new institutions with new concepts within which people can work, so it may be wise not to phase out the old system too quickly, while the new one is still struggling to survive. The PRC's experience with financial reform has been to dismantle the old system gradually, and at the same time build up a new one, so that the new system has grown from the old, and although it has some features of the old, it is no longer the old. Probably well into the future, direct control in the financial sector will not be phased out, not because we like it very much, but simply because it is still effective in maintaining financial stability. What is important is not the instrument used, but financial stability, and until we can confidently use indirect methods to ensure financial stability, we cannot completely abandon the direct tools that are still effective.

While much has been achieved with respect to financial sector reform over the last 17 years, what is ahead will be even more challenging to the authorities. The main challenges now are to keep a high savings rate, and therefore higher investment and growth rates, in the context of a market environment; to use indirect instruments to maintain macroeconomic stability; and to develop a market-friendly legal system and, more importantly, reinforce and implement these laws. None of these challenges and questions have an easy answer, but it is not possible to retreat on the road to financial reform. The PRC must continue to strive for a new financial system based on the principles of a socialist market economy.

CHAPTER FOUR

FINANCIAL SECTOR LIBERALIZATION AND REFORM: THE EXPERIENCE OF INDONESIA

SOEDRADJAD DJIWANDONO

As we move toward the end of the twentieth century, the world economy continues to undergo profound changes that are neither seasonal nor cyclical but rather fundamental or structural in nature. These changes have been taking place since the collapse of the Bretton Woods System or world monetary arrangements in 1971, characterized by the abolition of fixed exchange rates. Countries throughout the world, including the Republic of Indonesia, have suffered severe economic shocks. But together with the increased uncertainty generated by these changes has also come increased competition among economies, worldwide.

With rising competition and uncertainty worldwide, there is no alternative for many countries, especially the developing ones, but to embark on structural adjustments to gain a competitive edge. This common phenomenon has forced many developing countries to move toward greater reliance on market mechanisms. Adjustment policies introduced by governments have been driven by the objective of fostering a climate in which the business community can compete in a global environment marked by increasing uncertainty and fierce competition.

Structural adjustment includes broad objectives such as financial sector reform, monetary policy restructuring, price and fiscal reform, foreign exchange and trade system reform, industrial and other real sector restructuring. The breadth of reforms needed is closely associated with, and reflected by, economic indicators. Because the target and the course of adjustments for liberalization are somewhat different in individual countries, each country tends to have different policy needs underlying its particular target and the urgency to reach that target.

Since the latter part of the 1970s, governments in many developing countries have expressed their commitment to improve the allocation and mobilization of domestic resources through financial reforms. Prior to liberalization, financial systems in most developing countries were repressed through a variety of controls that did not reflect market forces, such as controls on interest rates and domestic credit, segmented and underdeveloped financial markets, restrictions on international capital flows, and excessive regulations. The move toward financial liberalization in many developing countries, therefore, showed the political will of governments to reduce the excessive regulations that had substantially discouraged financial savings. By liberalizing the financial sector, funds could be mobilized and resources allocated more efficiently in order to finance the bulk of investment needed for economic development.

This paper addresses Indonesia's experience in reforming the financial sector. It begins with the underlying conditions that existed prior to the reforms. It also presents the results and the lessons we have learned so far.

FINANCIAL REFORMS IN INDONESIA

Since the early 1970s, the external environment has been changing considerably, leading to increased uncertainty and competition in the world economy. In facing this environment, Indonesia has started to systematically build all the essential elements that would provide a basis for sustainable economic development. Adjustment policies have therefore been undertaken in all areas necessary to bring about sustainable economic growth, with particular emphasis on pricing policy, tax reform, export promotion, and financial sector reform. Since a government usually has many targets and objectives, all with different priorities, it is impossible to address them all with only one policy. Therefore, adjustment policies adopted in Indonesia were combined into packages that addressed multisectoral objectives that were related and compatible in nature. This necessitated prioritizing a long list of policies and targets, which were phased according to their urgency, based on careful consideration of the underlying conditions in the economy.

Conditions Prior to Financial Reform

In 1966, the *New Order* administration in Indonesia launched an economic stabilization and rehabilitation program aimed at reducing inflation and ensuring a sufficient supply of basic necessities. At the same time, the administration also started to reconstruct infrastructure and to adopt policies to support export growth and capacity. Prior to the reign of the *New Order*, the economic conditions in Indonesia reflected the efforts of a government preoccupied with political rather than economic issues. The poor performance of the Indonesian economy was demonstrated by an accelerating inflation rate that reached 635 percent in 1966 while, at the same time, the economy was only averaging a growth rate of 2.8 percent per annum. In the external sector, imports continued to increase while exports declined, with a resulting depletion of foreign exchange reserves, which was irrevocable without change.

The liberalization pioneered by the *New Order* and carried out in stages was prompted by changes in internal as well as by external conditions. The first stage of the economic reform (1970s) was part of the new initiative of the *New Order* government, which implemented economic stabilization policies by, inter alia, adopting a balanced budget policy, opening up the economy to foreign and domestic investment activities, and eliminating foreign exchange controls. Deliberate campaigns were launched to adopt development plans with the introduction of the Five-year Development Plans (called Repelitas), the first of which started in fiscal year 1969/70 and ended in 1973/74. The Long-term Plan phase one ended five periods of Repelitas that lasted up to 1993/94 and phase two of the Long-term Plan started in 1994/95.

The Indonesian economy was very dependent on oil revenue in the 1970s and early 1980s. The oil boom substantially influenced the rise in GDP growth in the 1979-1981 period to an average of 8.9 percent per annum, and this situation discouraged the government from deregulating. With worldwide recession in the early 1980s, Indonesia's economic growth fell to 2.3 percent while, at the same time, pressure on the balance of payments was brought about by unfavorable international oil prices. The fall in the oil price diminished the role of the government and the public sector as the engine of economic growth and, as a result, the government had to reschedule large government projects. The adverse impact of these events was reflected in a drastic decline in foreign exchange earnings and government revenues, which in turn contributed to lower imports and investment, leading to a slowdown in Indonesia's economic growth.

Major Aspects of the Adjustments

Structural adjustments in Indonesia, as noted earlier, covered all essential elements of the economy and encompassed not only macroeconomic management, but also micro and sectoral elements. On the macro side, Indonesia has, over the last 25 years, introduced policies to reduce uncertainty and maintain macroeconomic stability, thereby imposing the necessary discipline for a sound macroeconomic foundation. This comprised, first, fiscal policy with the goal of increasing government revenues and reducing expenditures by taking steps to simplify the tax system, reduce subsidies, and ensure efficient expenditure in order to sustain a dynamic balanced budget; and, second, prudent and consistent monetary policy. Prudent monetary policies included measures to safeguard price stability in terms of both domestic prices and the exchange rate. Policies were also adopted to bring about a more sustainable current account of the balance of payments, to manage external debt, and to develop a borrowing strategy, as well as to maintain sufficient foreign exchange reserves. Fiscal and monetary policies were carried out with the objective of providing an appropriate framework for a market-oriented economy. Indonesia's main goal over the past two decades has thus been to build a stable macroeconomic environment that would provide sustainable, non-inflationary growth.

The above reforms had to be accompanied by equally important measures on the micro side. Here measures were aimed at increasing the effectiveness and efficiency of various government units. The government also had to support and promote a climate conducive to business by improving and encouraging human resource development through training, education, supervision as well as institutional advancement.

Both macro and micro adjustment measures were crucial for Indonesia to tackle increasing competition and uncertainty; nevertheless, they also had to be complemented by sectoral adjustments. Sectoral economic policies can be differentiated into policies toward the real sector, including production (manufacturing, agriculture, etc.), the distribution sector (trade and services), and the banking sector and capital markets. The goal of sectoral measures was to increase the effectiveness and efficiency, and hence the competitiveness, of all sectors in the economy, including the financial sector. Policies were designed to eliminate overregulation of the economy by reducing government controls and by relying more on market mechanisms. Nonetheless, government intervention was still used if and where conditions necessitated it.

The Essence of Financial Adjustments

Indonesia, like other developing countries, is facing a gap between limited savings and increasing investment needs, and financial sector development is needed to improve intermediation between depositors and investors. Therefore, efforts to adjust the financial sector are focusing on enhancing the strategic function of banks and other financial institutions to support economic development. Reforms in the financial sector constitute an integral part of overall adjustment and development policies.

On the whole, adjustment policies in the financial sector reflect a consistent intention to achieve at least three basic objectives: first, to move toward a predominantly market-based financial system; second, to provide effective protection to the general public so that they can benefit from the services offered by the financial system; and third, to build an efficient and strong financial system that can support stable and healthy economic growth.

In the banking sector, liberalization measures started in June 1983, when the government announced its first serious deregulatory effort by allowing interest rates to rely more on market mechanisms and banks to determine their own deposit and lending rates. Formerly, interest rates of state banks for both deposits and loans were determined by Bank Indonesia (BI). Since state banks held the largest market share (60 percent), all interest rates were virtually determined by BI. These regulated rates were often too low to encourage domestic savings. After June 1983, interest rate determination was left to each bank's discretion and banks relied more on market forces, thereby becoming more attractive to depositors. Concurrently, BI lifted the credit ceiling and introduced monetary instruments, namely Bank Indonesia Certificates in 1984 and Money Market Securities in 1985, which were used as indirect monetary controls.

The process of liberalization in the financial sector was continued when, in October 1988, the government released its most important deregulation package to date, one which fundamentally changed the face of banking in Indonesia. *PAKTO*, as the package came to be known, removed the restrictions on new private banks, which had been in force since 1971. All limits on domestic bank branches were removed. Foreign banks were permitted to form joint ventures with local partners. The foreign partner could hold a maximum of 85 percent share and the new banks had to have a minimum paid-up capital requirement of $30 million. Existing foreign banks in Jakarta were allowed to branch out to six major provincial cities. State-owned enterprises were given leave to place up to 50 percent of their deposits outside state banks. This gave private banks a glimpse of an enormous, previously off-limits, pool of deposits and, at the same time, forced state banks to compete for deposits. BI imposed legal lending limits, which restricted a bank's aggregate amount of loans and advances to 20 percent of bank capital for any customer, and to 50 percent of bank capital for any one group of companies with common ownership. These limits were designed not only to prevent banks from being overexposed to a limited client base but also to drive large business conglomerates to seek market-based financing from a range of financial institutions.

BI has also taken steps to liberalize the capital markets with the aim of creating an environment conducive to investors as well as maintaining investor confidence. In December 1987 and December 1988, the government introduced measures to energize the capital market that had slumbered through the previous decade. The previous regulation limiting daily price swings to 4 percent of the price of a stock was abolished and foreigners were allowed to buy some shares. Foreign security houses were also given the green light to form joint ventures with local partners. The sudden emergence of competition from equity markets in 1989 had a profound effect on how banks marketed themselves to customers.

These measures encouraged more advanced banking activities as reflected in a number of banking indicators, such as the number of banks in operation as well as the value of funds mobilized and loans extended. As this growth was taking place, the Indonesian authorities remained concerned about the importance of maintaining macroeconomic stability, since Indonesia's long experience with reform had shown that macro management was a necessary condition to support economic development. In January 1990, the credit system was further improved by streamlining liquidity credits to three priority areas: food procurement, cooperatives, and investment. The policy was aimed at lowering inflationary pressures and excess liquidity (which might have had unfavorable affects on mobilizing savings) and at improving the credit structure, through removing distortions in market mechanisms by allowing more market-oriented interest rates. The measures also increased efficiency in the allocation of funds, promoted the role of banks in managing and carrying out the national credit system, and enhanced BI's role in monetary control.

Steps to increase prudential measures were considered to be equally important and, continuing with its prudential efforts to create a sound banking system, BI introduced a new set of measures at the end of February 1991. These measures included the introduction of capital adequacy requirements for banks, and encouraged banks to improve their management strategy and operational systems. The New Banking Act, which provided a legal foundation for responsible banking management that included the rights and obligations of related parties, was also introduced at the end of March 1992. To enforce the new Act, a series of government regulations concerning the operation of commercial banks, rural credit banks, and profit-sharing banks were issued, which further strengthened efforts to promote sound banking, and to provide guidelines for their operations. To assist banks to continue with prudential principles, BI updated the improved New Open Position (NOP) regulations in September 1994, which eased the NOP limit for transactions up to 25 percent of bank capital, for both balance sheet and off-balance sheet transactions. Banks were therefore given more leeway to make the necessary adjustments in their open positions.

ASSESSMENTS AND LESSONS

The Results

The entire deregulation or adjustment program adopted by Indonesia has been very fruitful as evidenced by many economic indicators. For more than a decade, the Indonesian economy has registered relatively high growth rates averaging 6.9 percent per annum. This strong economic growth has enabled incomes to rise considerably and has resulted in Indonesia graduating to a "lower middle income" country. These favorable figures have been supported by other factors: first, the increasingly important role of the manufacturing sector in supporting economic growth; second, the dominant role of non-oil/gas exports whose value has jumped from 25 percent to more than 75 percent of total export earnings over the past decade; third, within the government budget, the increasing proportion of non-oil revenue to total domestic revenue, which has surged from less than 30 percent to around 76 percent. With the bulk of the non-oil government revenue coming from taxes, Indonesia has built greater financial independence. The growing prominence of the private sector also reflects the diminishing role of the government.

In line with other positive results from the adjustment measures, the outcome from the financial reformation has also been impressive. Indonesia's banking industry recorded a dynamic advancement, both in terms of the number of banks or offices and in terms of the mobilization of financial sources. At the end of 1995, Indonesia had a total of 240 banks with more than 6,000 bank offices, compared with October 1988 when there were about 124 banks and about 1,900 bank offices. Over the same period, funds mobilized by banks reached US$87 billion with total bank loans of US$97 billion, compared with the previous US$22 billion and US$25 billion, respectively. Meanwhile, the capital market has grown rapidly as illustrated by the dramatic increase in the number of companies listed in the Jakarta Stock Exchange—from 24 in December 1988 to 236 in September 1995, with the volume of stocks rising from 72 million shares to 45 billion shares and the value of market capitalization rising from US$275 million to US$62.5 billion. Foreign investors have played an important part in the development of the capital market. All of these developments have linked the domestic market to the international market.

More importantly, financial reforms have also led to more effective market mechanisms within the banking system, thus enhancing the function of the banking system as a financial intermediary. Efforts toward deregulating the banking industry, for example, have led to increased competition among banks, prompting, in turn, greater efficiency. Banks are now more independent in terms of being able to set their own business strategies. They have become more market-oriented, as reflected in interest rates for both deposits and loans, and they have introduced a variety of new financial products. With the introduction of commercial paper, bank financing, and other forms of financing, the business community has now gone beyond traditional bank lending. Greater dependence on market forces has allowed, and will continue to allow, Indonesia's financial markets to operate more effectively in terms of mobilizing and allocating financial resources.

The Lessons

The initial conditions in an economy determine the form and scope of adjustment policies. Steps that are pursued in one country may not necessarily be applicable to other countries, and likewise, the objectives that will be achieved by adjustment policies will differ across countries. Therefore, the terms that are used to exemplify adjustment frequently vary from one country to another. The term "structural adjustment" is used in developed countries, "economic reforms" describes the process in previously socialist and communist countries, and "deregulations/ debureaucratization" is used in developing countries, including

Indonesia. Even within a country or an economy, the form of adjustment policies may vary from time to time because of changes that occur in the economy. In Indonesia, for instance, the high economic costs of bureaucracy, relatively widespread government, and regulations in various sectors of the economy constituted the initial conditions, and the form of adjustment policies pursued thus far has been deregulation and debureaucratization. However, this does not mean that reregulation is out of the question in the future, especially in view of the structural changes that may occur with the advancement of the economy and the modernization of the financial sector.

On the question of the sequencing of adjustment policies, various models and numerous arguments have been advanced in the literature as to which sector should be liberalized first: real versus monetary sector, monetary versus fiscal, money market versus capital market, and trade liberalization either preceding, being adopted simultaneously with, or following financial reforms. McKinnon argues that adjustments should not be undertaken simultaneously, but should be properly sequenced. The validity of such arguments is, to a large context, determined by the initial conditions in an economy. It is difficult to make generalizations since economic conditions in one country differ from those in other countries. Theories on sequencing often disregard preexisting conditions in a country and rarely provide sufficient alternatives for policy makers to decide on the optimal course of adjustment policies.

Indonesia's reform was a set of responsive actions taken by the authorities. However, every situation and condition is different so that no particular situation ever properly matches a set of necessary conditions that would provide the background against which a particular policy would be taken. Although theoretically a certain policy may appear suitable for a particular circumstance, in practice, the circumstances may not be appropriate for the underlying policy. In fact, given the dynamics of the problem, any authority has to move expeditiously to address the challenges adequately. It is even said that a difficult situation can produce good policy. When everything is fine and in order, there would be no urgency to consider new measures.

The basic principle in this sequencing approach, therefore, is not how to justify the political decision to reform the financial sector or the real sector, but what the underlying circumstances of the overall economy are at the time. The motivation behind, and the determination to proceed with, reform is the need to remedy the weaknesses in an economy that is not able to keep up with international progress.

Another lesson learned from financial reformation in Indonesia pertains to the removal of barriers to entry into the banking industry in a very abrupt manner, as stipulated in the 1988 decree, which can produce quite an astonishing impact on the banking industry—both positive and negative—as well as on the overall economy. Indeed in Indonesia, the freeing up of the banking sector resulted in significant advances in the sector. Banks were induced to find new methods to mobilize funds and at the same time to extend new loans. This, to a large extent, contributed to the upswing in the economy. But it led to the problem of economic overheating. On the micro management side, the growing credit extended by banks due, in part, to the oversupply of funds, produced a bad debt problem, which emerged in the following years. It seems, in retrospect, that the reformation was somewhat too fast and too soon. The tremendous expansion in the banking industry over the period 1989 to 1991 was not accompanied by an appropriate level of compliance to prudent banking principles. In dealing with this problem, corrective measures were taken in 1991 to prevent further deterioration in the industry.

This experience suggests that although Indonesia's financial reformation was instrumental in promoting the banking industry, nonetheless, the timing of implementation proved to be crucial and critical in determining the outcome. The main lesson learned in this context is that prudent banking principles should be established prior to financial reformation, or at least established in tandem with the reforms, and are a necessary condition for coping with increasing competition in the global arena. This is partly why Indonesia has, since 1991, focused more on maintaining prudential principles, not only in the banking industry, but also in economic management as a whole. There is a saying that it "takes two to tango"; in the case of financial reformation, it takes everything to achieve success. Prudent macro management needs concerted efforts in fiscal and monetary policies that are directly related to financial reformation. In addition, financial reform must also be supported impartially by overall structural adjustments in all the elements of the economy.

One common phenomenon arose as Indonesia deregulated many facets of the economy. Before deregulation, the government possessed a set of comprehensive tools and regulations by which to control economic activity. Similarly, the monetary authority had a complete set of "dos" and "don'ts" to manage and influence the banking sector and monetary behavior. Since financial adjustment measures were basically designed to deregulate most elements of monetary and banking activity, the ownership of instruments and regulation by the authority have diminished over time. Therefore, a particular regulatory instrument, namely moral suasion, has taken on greater importance. For monetary management to be successful, BI had to go beyond managing the growth of reserve money through normal open market operations, and include steps to contain the growth of monetary aggregates. Since bank credit expansion was the main factor that contributed toward the growth of monetary aggregates, Indonesia persisted in moral suasion programs to influence banks in their lending activities.

Regular monthly meetings with the banking sector have been an important measure for encouraging moral suasion. At those meetings, BI provided a macro picture of the economy and raised some critical issues for banks to take into consideration, especially signs of emerging economic overheating. BI also shared with banks selected data showing the currently vulnerable sectors in order to persuade banks to readjust their lending activities to those sectors. Banks were also asked to submit their credit plans and BI discussed with them the consequences of their credit expansion plans on both macroeconomic stability and their financial condition. Through these steps, BI has tried to achieve better and sounder macroeconomic management through implementation of prudential principles by banks, and through a program that has linked macro and micro management and has relied on better coordination between the central bank and the banking community.

The deregulation measures adopted in Indonesia were aimed at streamlining regulations. However, this did not necessarily mean that the authorities were going to set up a free system. In fact, at certain stages, and if necessary, new regulations might be imposed to produce a sound and efficient banking system. However, the authorities have also learned that regulations in themselves are not enough to ensure sound banking operations. The effectiveness of regulations depends on management by the banks themselves. Regardless of how well regulations are designed, a regulation might still contain loopholes that could be exploited to evade compliance. Therefore, BI requires banks to adopt stricter self-regulatory principles by taking into account the risks that might arise in the course of business. Applying self-regulatory principles helps ensure that banks do not conduct their operations solely on the basis of what is permitted in general regulations but, more importantly, that they apply internal regulations that specify a detailed application of general regulations.

CHAPTER FIVE

INNOVATIONS IN FINANCIAL SECTOR REFORM IN NEW ZEALAND

DONALD T. BRASH

BACKGROUND

The context in which New Zealand came to revise or review its banking supervision arrangements is one component of substantial and sweeping economic reforms since the mid-1980s that covered almost every aspect of the economy, the tax system protection, the government sector, and so on. In the macro area, New Zealand saw fiscal policy resulting in a move from a deficit of 7 percent of GDP in the mid-1980s to a surplus of 4 percent of GDP currently. It is hardly surprising with that background that New Zealand has also seen very far-reaching changes in both financial sector and monetary policy.

In the decades prior to 1984, New Zealand was in many ways the worst performing economy in the OECD, with very slow growth, relatively high inflation, and very large fiscal and current account deficits. In the financial sector prior to the mid-1980s, interest rates were subject to government control and the banking market was closed to all except the existing four banks (one government-owned, three foreign-owned). Banks were at various times subject to guidelines as to which sectors they could invest in. There were tight controls on the outward remittances of foreign exchange on capital account and some (fairly tight) restrictions on inward foreign investment, and a fixed exchange rate.

In July 1984, a severe foreign exchange crisis, coupled with the election of a new Labor Government, prompted a very extensive change in policy across almost every aspect of the economy. Reforms included the complete abolition of all import quotas and a substantial (and unilateral) reduction in tariffs; the complete removal of all controls on wages, prices, rents, and dividends; and substantial reform of the labor market. The taxation system was overhauled, with the top marginal rate of personal income tax cut from 66 percent to 33 percent, and a comprehensive value-added tax was introduced. Subsidies for both agriculture and manufacturing were removed and a program of extensive privatization of government-owned trading operations was introduced

By 1986, all interest rate controls had been removed. There was a freely floating exchange rate (and I think it is true to say that New Zealand is the only country in the world that has not intervened directly in its foreign exchange market for more than 11 years now). There were absolutely no restrictions on the outward remittances of capital and virtually no restrictions on inward foreign investment. There were no "guidelines" telling banks where they should lend and there were no requirements for banks to hold deposits with the central bank. New Zealanders were free to write contracts in any currency of their choice (though they were, and remain, obliged to pay tax in New Zealand dollars). The banking market had been thrown wide open to any number of banks, locally incorporated or otherwise, subject only to basic qualitative criteria relating to prudential soundness. Instead of 4 banks, we quite quickly had 21.

In monetary policy, change was equally dramatic. Prior to the mid-1980s, monetary policy was targeted at multiple objectives—price stability, full employment, economic growth, balance of payments equilibrium, etc. The central bank was also under the close control of government, with the Reserve Bank of New Zealand (RBNZ) being consistently rated among the least independent in the world over that period. The outcome, as mentioned, was inflation which, while not high by the standards of, say, Latin America or Eastern Europe, was quite poor as far as the standards of the OECD were concerned (consistently above 10 percent through most of the seventies and early eighties).

Starting in mid-1984 in practice, and from early 1990 after a change in the law, RBNZ was made responsible for achieving the single objective of price stability; the objective was explicitly defined in a written, public agreement between the Government and the Governor. The Governor was required to keep inflation as measured by the Consumer Price Index between 0 and 2 percent for every 12 monthly period (the definition of inflation excludes such things as changes in indirect taxation and major international price shocks).[1] The Governor was given full independence to operate monetary policy as he judged appropriate, but with the quid pro quo that at least every six months, he had to report to Parliament on progress in the implementation of policy and could be dismissed for "inadequate performance" under the inflation target agreement. The result has been that, for the last five years, we kept the inflation rate as defined in the agreement.

A NEW APPROACH TO BANKING SUPERVISION

In this context, it is hardly surprising that RBNZ decided to conduct a full review of how we were conducting banking supervision, starting in November 1991. Prior to this, and from the time the banking sector had been opened up to new banks, we had been performing banking supervision along conventional Basle Committee lines. The review was motivated by three concerns: first, both the compliance and efficiency costs of increasingly intensive bank supervision; second, the risk to the taxpayer from the traditional approach to supervision, which is based on the supervisor, with only the supervisor knowing the detailed prudential state of the banking system; and third, whether instead of reducing the risks in the banking system we were increasing them by reducing the incentives for bank directors and bank managers to monitor their own operations and make their own judgments about what constitutes prudent

---

[1] The target inflation rate was revised subsequent to the ADB seminar.

behavior. These concerns were based on looking at other countries like the United States and Japan.

Our new approach, which came into operation in January 1996, involves a combination of regulation and disclosure. We are not removing all regulation as some have described, but are significantly reducing the extent of regulation, a move which we believe is made possible by the adoption of a comprehensive and rigorous disclosure regime. It gives us one of the least regulated banking systems in the world. However, we are confident that the new structure will prove at least as successful in promoting a sound and successful financial system as the more conventional approaches to banking supervision do, and probably with considerably lower compliance costs and lower taxpayer risk.

The key features of the framework are as follows:

- A new set of public disclosure requirements obliges all banks to issue quarterly disclosure statements to the public. These statements are subject to two annual external audits by the bank's regular audit firm, although the half year audit is a limited review. No audit is carried out by the central bank. The disclosure statements required are comprehensive, covering the usual financial statements, as well as disclosures on all significant risk dimensions, a bank's credit rating and its systems for managing its business risks. These quarterly statements by definition will be long and therefore of interest primarily to market professionals. As a consequence, RBNZ is also requiring banks to publish a Key Information Summary (no more than two pages) each quarter for each branch.

- The new approach places greater emphasis on the role of the banks' directors. They are required to sign the disclosure statements each quarter, and are required to attest to the adequacy of their bank's internal control systems. Directors face severe criminal and civil penalties when a disclosure statement is false or misleading.

- Given the benefits of the new disclosure regime, RBNZ has withdrawn the internal control guidelines, which were introduced in 1992. Banks are therefore no longer subject to mandatory review of their internal control systems. We have removed the limit on the amount that a bank may lend to an individual borrower, but the quarterly disclosure statements do require banks to indicate how much risk concentration they have, by indicating how many individual counterparts exceed 20 percent of capital, how many 30 percent of capital, and so on. We have also removed the previous limit on open foreign exchange positions.

- RBNZ will continue to monitor banks but on the basis of their public disclosure statements. The previous quarterly prudential returns have been discontinued.

- We are retaining certain regulations, in particular the 8 percent, risk-weighted Basle capital framework. Although we believe that disclosure alone would ensure that banks would maintain at least equivalent to the 8 percent minimum, we consider that retention of the minimum capital requirements reinforces the credibility of the new supervisory framework, at no cost to the banks.

- We are retaining a limit on the amount that a bank may lend to a related party, such as a parent bank. We consider that disclosure alone is unlikely to be sufficient in all circumstances to ensure that a bank will not be coerced into lending to a related party, to the potential detriment of New Zealand's financial system.

- We are trying to ensure that, where practical, all regulatory requirements imposed on banks will be applied evenly and in a standardized way. All such requirements will be publicly disclosed so as to facilitate market monitoring of a bank's compliance with the requirements and to increase their transparency.

RBNZ believes the new approach offers three major advantages. First, disclosure considerably strengthens the incentives for bank managers and directors to identify, monitor, and manage their own business risks. Second, disclosure places market pressures on banks to behave prudently. The strongest banks are going to find themselves able to operate at lower costs; weaker banks are going to be under pressure to strengthen their position. Third, disclosure reinforces the perception that the management and directors of a bank have the sole responsibility for the management of the bank's affairs, and eliminates the monopoly of information that supervisors tend to have in respect of a bank's financial condition. Regulation, by contrast, can create serious impediments to financial market innovation and efficiency. It can seriously reduce the incentives for the management and directors of banks to take responsibility for the management of their banks and can increase the risk of moral hazard.

Given that almost all of New Zealand's banks are owned outside New Zealand, a question is whether our proposed approach simply involves our freeloading on the more conventional approach to supervision maintained by other countries (particularly in our case the Reserve Bank of Australia, the Bank of England, and the Federal Reserve Board). Unfortunately, I cannot prove that our approach would have been politically feasible with a different ownership structure of our banks—any more than those who charge us with freeloading can prove the reverse.

But it is my firmly held conviction that we would be adopting this approach even if most of our banks had been locally owned. We believe, quite strongly, that the regime is more likely to promote prudent banking behavior than the conventional approach.

It is perhaps interesting to observe that the banks themselves are taking the new approach very seriously, and regard it with some real apprehension. That is especially true of the somewhat weaker banks, which have been able to take shelter within the previous system, which of course, tended to make all banks appear equal.

Some months ago, I had a visit from the CEO of one major international bank with an operation in New Zealand and he told me that he had come to protest strongly at the requirement that bank directors would have to sign off on the disclosure statements every quarter, and attest to the appropriateness of their risk control systems. When I asked why, he said, "Bank directors know absolutely nothing about banking." This comment is quite unfair about many bank directors, of course, but there is an uncomfortable element of truth in it in some cases. The blame for this situation almost certainly lies in part on a supervision regime that has assumed too much of the responsibility for the viability of banks. We very much hope that a regime that will continue to have some key regulations but which is based primarily around market disclosure and director attestations will improve that situation.

In short, we are convinced that the new system increases the incentives for prudent behavior, and so reduces the risk of bank failure. There should also be some reduction in taxpayer risk and in both compliance and efficiency costs.

CHAPTER SIX

PRESUMPTIVE INDICATORS OF VULNERABILITY TO FINANCIAL CRISES IN EMERGING ECONOMIES

MORRIS GOLDSTEIN

This paper discusses a set of presumptive indicators that should prove helpful to analysts in recognizing potential financial crises in emerging market economies. In brief, I have searched through the relevant literature and examined the lessons of the recent crises in emerging markets (especially the recent Mexican crisis) for external conditions and for borrowing-country policies and characteristics that seem to increase *vulnerability* to a financial crisis. The paper does not provide formal statistical tests of the forecasting properties of alternative early warning indicators. That should clearly be the next step in the research agenda. In the final section of the paper, I summarize the results of two recent empirical studies that make a useful start on such a forecasting exercise.

For our purposes, it is convenient to think of a financial crisis (along systemic risk lines) as the likelihood of a sudden, usually unexpected collapse of confidence in a significant portion of the banking or financial system—or in currency markets—with potentially large real economic effects.[1] For now, I will not draw dis-

---

[1] This is very close to the definition of systemic risk proposed by Ludwig (1994). The reason for defining financial crisis in terms of the "potential" to adversely affect the real economy is that public policy, particularly monetary policy and lender-of-last-resort actions, has the capability of averting the crisis—albeit at the cost of increasing other kinds of risks.

tinctions among various types of financial crises—be they foreign exchange crises, or banking crises, or debt crises.[2] In the Mexican case, all three of those elements were present. Although the focus is on financial crises in emerging markets, the paper frequently makes reference to financial crises in industrial countries as well—especially the European Exchange Rate Mechanism (ERM) crises in the fall of 1992 and the summer of 1993— since that experience is instructive. Finally, the emphasis is on crises that are precipitated, or exacerbated, by large shifts in international capital flows.

The rest of the paper is organized as follows. The following section takes up seven presumptive indicators of financial vulnerability in emerging markets. The seven deadly sins are (i) an upward turn in international interest rates; (ii) growing mismatch between the government's/banking system's short-term liquid liabilities and its liquid assets (particularly international reserves); (iii) a large current account deficit, used mainly for consumption and financed in good measure with short-term borrowing; (iv) a highly overvalued real exchange rate, exacerbated by the politicization of exchange rate policy decisions; (v) constraints (most of them related to financial fragility) on the willingness to increase domestic interest rates when there is an adverse shift in international capital flows; (vi) an unsustainable boom in bank lending followed by a sharp fall in asset prices (particularly equity and real estate prices); and (vii) high susceptibility to "contagion" (reflecting small country size, regional effects, characteristics similar to those of the original crisis country and/or weak policy fundamentals) following the outbreak of a financial crisis elsewhere.[3]

For each indicator, I offer a brief rationale, followed by a discussion of caveats and of issues of implementation. I also discuss the indicator's recent relevance, including reference to recent country examples. The analysis reveals that many of the

---

[2] For a discussion of different types of financial crises and their origins, see Schwartz (1986), Krugman (1991), Mishkin (1994), Eisenbeis (1995), Garber and Svensson (1995), Kaminisky and Reinhart (1996), and Goldstein (1995a); see also the concluding remarks in this paper.

[3] It should be conceded at the outset that there is some overlap among these seven indicators; nevertheless, the argument is that each indicator provides some useful information not captured by the others.

factors that have been linked to financial crises in industrial countries (e.g., overvalued real exchange rates, recession, sharp increases in interest rates, and stock market declines) also figure prominently in financial crises in emerging markets.[4] The paper concludes with some remarks on future directions for this type of research.

THE SEVEN DEADLY SINS

Interest in early warning signals of financial difficulties in emerging markets obviously owes much to the 1994/95 Mexican economic crisis. A problem, however, is that the Mexican crisis presented so many potential lessons about vulnerability to financial crises that it is difficult to identify which lessons are specific to Mexico and which are of wider applicability to other emerging market economies. For example, was Mexico particularly vulnerable to a crisis because of its relatively large current account deficit (nearly 8 percent of GDP in 1994), or because of the appreciated (overvalued) level of its real exchange rate, or because of the maturity (short-term) and currency composition (*tesobonos* [Mexican Government dollar-indexed bonds]) of its external debt, or because of the consumption/investment split of its foreign borrowing, or because of the February 1994 upward turn in the international interest rate cycle, or because of growing weaknesses in its domestic banking system? Probably it was all of the above. Likewise, one might ask whether in light of Mexico's experience, "stock" measures of financial vulnerability (e.g., the ratio of maturing external payments to international reserves) should be given more weight than "flow" measures (the ratio of the current account deficit to GDP), or whether some indicators that didn't flash very brightly in the Mexican case (e.g., currency or default risk implied by interest rate differentials) have a better track record in other crises.

This paper can only make a start in answering those questions; the subject is too broad—and the most relevant empirical evidence too recent and preliminary—to go beyond that. Never-

---

[4] For an analysis of these factors in the industrial-country context, see Mishkin (1994).

theless, by casting the net more widely rather than considering the Mexican experience alone, I believe it is possible to draw some useful conclusions for analysts studying and monitoring financial developments in emerging market economies. Seen in this context, the remainder of this section considers seven presumptive indicators or early warning signals that seem to have played a role in earlier financial crises.

An Upward Turn in International Interest Rates

A sharp increase in international interest rates[5] increases the vulnerability of emerging markets in at least three ways.

First, it makes investing in industrial countries more attractive at the margin than investing in emerging markets. This is the *asset substitution* channel. It implies that net private capital flows from industrial countries to emerging markets are likely to slow or to reverse themselves after a rise in industrial-country interest rates, as investors reallocate their portfolios to the new set of risks and returns.[6] If this change in net capital flows is large and unexpected, it can lead to serious adjustment problems in debtor countries: some bank loans and investment projects may have to be liquidated; absorption will need to fall relative to income; and monetary and fiscal policy will likely need to be tightened to bolster the confidence of investors. Economic growth will usually decline, at least temporarily. The more the borrowing country has overdone it by relying too heavily on capital inflows for financing and by investing the proceeds of foreign borrowing unproductively, the more serious are the consequences likely to be when these flows decline sharply.

---

[5] One can think of "international" interest rates as a weighted average of interest rates in the G-7 countries.

[6] Note that the rearranging of asset shares in response to a new pattern of interest rate differentials is a finite process. Suppose, for example, that industrial investors hold 96 percent of their portfolio in industrial-country assets and 4 percent in emerging market assets. Now assume that a rise in industrial-country interest rates reduces the optimal share of emerging market assets from 4 to 2 percent. While this adjustment is going on, net capital flows to emerging markets will be declining. But once that share reaches 2 percent, the adjustment process will cease (in the absence of further changes in interest rates). From that point on, the investor will acquire emerging market assets equal to 2 percent of the growth of the total portfolio. See Fernandez-Arias and Montiel (1995) for further discussion of this stock-adjustment effect.

Second, an increase in international interest rates impacts adversely on the *creditworthiness* of emerging market borrowers. Not only does it increase the present discounted value of contractual debt payments (where external debt carries floating interest rates), but it also reduces the presented discounted value of the resources available to make external payments; higher interest rates reduce the debtor's ability to pay.

Third, high interest rates can exacerbate *information and moral hazard problems* in credit markets. When interest rates rise, so too will the probability that lenders will lend to bad credit risks because it is the individuals, firms, and countries with the riskiest investment projects that will be most willing to pay the highest interest rates. Lenders may respond to this adverse selection problem by rationing credit to what they perceive to be low-quality borrowers. Mishkin (1994), for example, concludes that increases in interest rates were one of the key factors promoting financial crises in the United States (US) during the 1857-1991 period, and one might expect a similar deterioration in the functioning of international credit markets following periods of large increases in interest rates.

Consistent with these a priori arguments, available empirical studies suggest that movements in international interest rates—especially US rates—are capable of explaining much of the well-documented surge in private capital inflows to developing countries in the 1990s. Recall that short-term nominal interest rates in the US fell from over 7.5 percent in 1990 to about 3 percent in 1993, as the Federal Reserve eased monetary policy to spur recovery from the recession. It was not until February 1994 that US short-term interest rates began to move in the other direction. Taken as a group, empirical studies conclude that foreign financial variables accounted for more than half (and sometimes as much as 85 percent) of the capital inflow surge and three quarters or more of the variation in secondary market prices of developing-countries bank debt.[7] As shown in Figure 6.1 (where private capital flows are proxied by international re-

---

[7] See Calvo et al (1993), Fernandez-Arias (1994), Dooley et al (1994), Frankel (1995), and Goldstein (1995b); Chuhan et al (1993) find that external financial conditions were more important for flows to Latin America than for those to Asia.

Figure 6.1   Mexican Reserves and United States Interest Rates

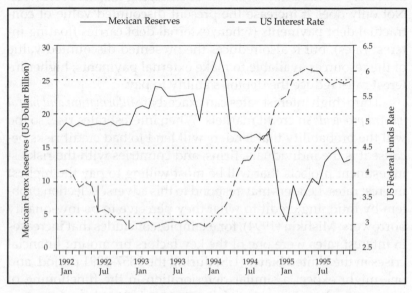

Source: International Financial Statistics

serves), net private capital flows to Mexico were related inversely to movements in US interest rates in the early 1990s.

Analysts can get a picture of the market's expectation about interest rates in creditor countries from futures market quotations and from the term structure of interest rates. For illustrative purposes, the top panel of Figure 6.2 indicates how market participants, during the April-October 1995 period, revised their expectations about the future course of US interest rates. Whereas in April 1995 the expectation was that short rates in the first quarter of 1996 would hover around 7 percent, by June 1995 that expectation had been revised downward to just over 5 percent; in the fall of 1995, it had risen to about 5.5 percent. The bottom panel of Figure 6.2 illustrates that the term structure of US rates shifted down, and became much flatter, between January 1995 and January 1996—a development that was generally shared across the G-7 countries and that no doubt contributed to a more buoyant net flow of private capital to emerging markets in 1995 than most observers had expected in the wake of the Mexican crisis.

In *sum*, the message for analysts is that emerging market countries become more vulnerable both to a drop-off in private capital

Figure 6.2   Market Expectations of United States Interest Rates

Panel A.   Projected Interest Rates Based on Futures Market Quotations
(three-month interest rates in percent per annum)

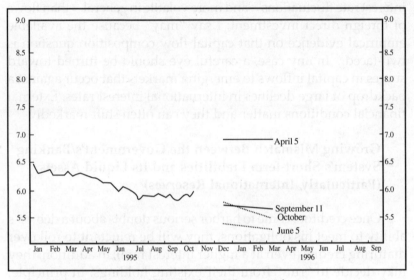

Note: Data from January 1995 to October 1995 are actuals.

Panel B. Yield Curves

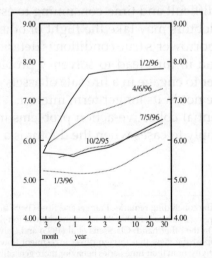

Note: Yields on treasury bills and government bonds of varying maturities.

Source: Bloomberg Financial Markets

inflows and to financial crisis when there is a large actual or prospective increase in international interest rates. Vulnerability will be highest for those host countries with relatively high external debt burdens. Vulnerability may also be larger for host countries that have relied heavily on portfolio capital flows (bonds and equities) since these flows are often regarded as more sensitive to interest rate fluctuations—and more volatile in general—than flows of foreign direct investment; I say "may" because the available empirical evidence on that capital flow composition question is two-faced.[8] In any case, a careful eye should be turned toward surges in capital inflows to emerging markets that occur against a backdrop of large declines in international interest rates. External financial conditions matter and they can often shift markedly.

Growing Mismatch Between the Government's/Banking System's Short-term Liabilities and Its Liquid Assets (Particularly, International Reserves)[9]

Once creditors come to harbor serious doubts about a debtor's ability to meet his obligations, they will be reluctant to roll over maturing credits (even at a higher interest rate); in addition, they may decide to "run" from their existing holdings. In principle, creditors ought to be willing to see beyond illiquidity problems and continue to support a solvent borrower; in practice, however, it can be difficult and time-consuming to establish proof of solvency and debtors may take the flight of other creditors as a signal that the borrower's true condition is deteriorating. Liquidity problems can in turn lead to solvency problems by forcing the debtor either to engage in a fire sale of assets or to undertake policies that are not in its longer term interest.

These potential collective-action problems in private credit markets also apply to cases when the debtor is a government or

---

[8] As reported in the concluding remarks, Frankel and Rose (1995) find that vulnerability to currency crises in emerging markets is higher the lower the share of foreign direct investment in total capital inflows. On the other hand, Claessens et al (1993) and Calvo and Reinhart (1996) report results that support the view that foreign direct investment flows are little different in their interest rate sensitivity, or in their time-series behavior more generally, from portfolio flows.

[9] The arguments and country references included in this subsection are developed more fully in Calvo and Goldstein (1996).

a private bank. Suppose the government has a large amount of short-term foreign-currency-denominated debt coming due relative to its stock of international reserves. Creditors will recognize that unlike the situation with debt denominated in domestic currency, the central bank cannot ease the government's liquidity problem by printing currency and supplying it to the government. If the existing stock of international reserves is inadequate (to meet maturing obligations), foreign exchange would have to be borrowed (probably from other central banks). Also, a devaluation will not lower the government's foreign-currency-denominated obligations; it will reduce the need for further borrowing and permit the debtor to earn foreign exchange in the future. But the shorter the time horizon and the larger the existing "stock" disequilibrium, the less useful will be "flow" remedies. Because few governments in either developed or industrial countries are prepared to allow large financial institutions to fail, bank liabilities too may be regarded as (contingent) liabilities of the government (if the banking system is weak). For all these reasons, a *rising gap between a government's short-term debt obligations and its stock of international reserves* can generate the loss of confidence that initiates a financial crisis.

Turning to *banks*, they have several characteristics that make them particularly susceptible to runs. Bank loans are both illiquid and difficult to evaluate. Banks' other assets (mortgages and bonds) have long maturities and often fixed interest rates as well. Meanwhile, banks operate with high leverage (low capital) and on a fractional reserve basis (relatively small amounts of cash), and their funding is short term. Deposits are redeemable *at par*. Not everyone will be able to withdraw funds at the same time. There is thus an incentive to be at the front of the line at the first hint of trouble. A negative shock to one bank may lead depositors to suspect that *all* banks have become more risky, and it may be easier to withdraw funds now than to engage in a costly information search (especially if publicly available information on individual banks is thin). Recall too that capital market liberalization has made it easier and less costly for residents of emerging markets to move their assets out of the country when they sense that a large change in the risk/return outlook is in the offing. Foreign-currency-denominated bank liabilities (often introduced to reduce the incentives for capital flight) are now sub-

stantial in many emerging markets. Bank capital, deposit insurance, and the existence of a lender of last resort can each serve to
boost confidence and discourage bank runs—but the capital/
insurance cushion is not large in most emerging markets and a
fixed (or quasi-fixed) exchange rate can tightly circumscribe the
central bank's ability to extend emergency financial assistance.
Thus, here too, a rising gap between short-term liabilities and
liquid assets is apt to make financial markets nervous.

Reference to the timing of the Mexican crisis and the pattern
of attacks across emerging market economies reinforces the relevance of such maturity and currency mismatches. As part of the
effort to limit the rise in domestic interest rates that would otherwise have ensued from a decline in private capital flows into
Mexico in early 1994, the Mexican authorities engaged in a large-
scale substitution of lower yielding, foreign-currency indexed
tesobonos for higher yielding, Mexican Government peso-denominated bonds (*cetes*). Between February and November 1994, the
stock of *tesobonos* expanded by nearly tenfold. This was occurring at the same time that Mexico's stock of international reserves
was declining rapidly. By end September, the former had already
come to exceed the latter, and by the beginning of December
(only a few weeks before the crisis), the gap was on the order of
$10 billion.[10] A similar picture emerges if we compare a more
aggregate measure of short-term government debt (the stock of
tesobonos plus the stock of *cetes*) to Mexico's gross international
reserves (see Figure 6.3). The gap becomes progressively larger
from the second quarter of 1994 on, and widens appreciably in
October and November.

Figure 6.4 brings a cross-country perspective to the same type
of public debt early warning signal. Specifically, it shows scheduled public debt service (first excluding, then including debt
amortization) as a share of exports for four emerging market countries in Latin America over the period 1992-1994.[11] Note that by
this indicator, Mexico was much more vulnerable to attack in

---

[10] By way of contrast, during 1995 Mexico reduced its outstanding stock of *tesobonos* by
99 percent, and added significantly to its stock of international reserves; see U.S. Treasury
(1995).

[11] The picture would be qualitatively similar if we substituted international reserves
for exports.

Figure 6.3   Mexico: Domestic Debt[a] (in US Dollars) and International Reserves

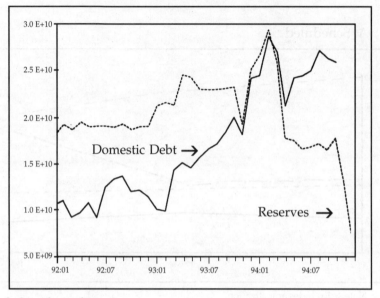

[a]   *Cetes* plus *tesobonos.*

1994 than either Chile or Argentina.[12] On this count, Brazil looks about as vulnerable in 1994 as Mexico; the fact that it didn't get attacked first or simultaneously may have something to do with the fact that Brazilian debt (outside the central bank) was largely in the hands of Brazilian commercial banks and firms that were less yield conscious than holders of Mexican *tesobonos.*

Figure 6.5 provides an analogous picture of maturity/currency mismatch on the banking side for Mexico. In this case, the indicator examined is a broad measure of bank liabilities (monetary aggregate) relative to the stock of international reserves. Specifically, Figure 6.5 charts the evolution of Mexican M2 deflated by the peso/dollar exchange rate (labeled M2$), along with Mexico's gross international reserves. Beginning in 1989, the gap between the two widens progressively; observe that just before

---

[12] Both the level and change in the debt ratio are probably relevant.

Figure 6.4   Public Sector Debt Service (Foreign and Domestic)/Exports Ratio in Selected Countries, 1992-1994

A. Scheduled

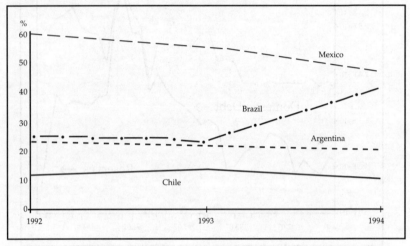

Note: Excludes amortization.

B. Potential

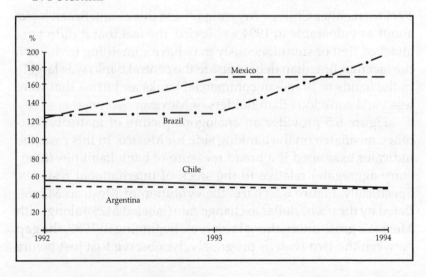

Note: Includes amortization.
Source: Calvo and Goldstein (1996).

Figure 6.5   Mexico: M2 (in US Dollars) and International Reserves

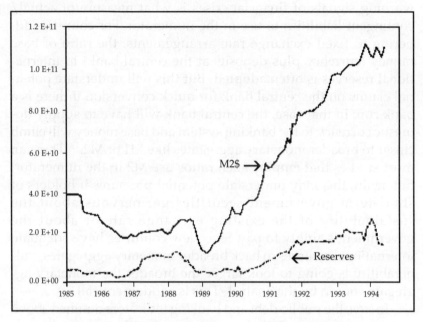

Source: Calvo and Goldstein (1996).

the December 20 devaluation, M2$ had climbed to a level almost 5 times higher than the maximum level of international reserves ever recorded in Mexico. By way of comparison with Mexico's ratio of 5, the corresponding ratios for Brazil and Chile were around 3 and 1.5, respectively—again pointing to Mexico's higher vulnerability. The relevant indicator for Argentina (M3 relative to international reserves) takes on a high value—not much different from Mexico's.

In gauging the relative vulnerability of the banking system across countries, one should also factor in (as suggested above), the type of exchange arrangements in force; on this score, Mexico (with its quasi-fixed rate) and Argentina (with its currency board) were more vulnerable than Brazil and Chile because the former two countries' exchange arrangements provided less latitude for the central bank to act as lender of last resort. Interestingly enough, both Mexico and Argentina had to arrange outside official support packages in 1995 to alleviate problems in their banking systems.

The thorniest part of using liability-to-asset ratios as early warning signals of financial crises is what measure of actual/contingent liabilities to use in the numerator. For countries adhering to fixed exchange rate arrangements, the ratio of base money (currency plus deposits at the central bank) to international reserves is often adopted. But this will understate potential claims on the central bank for quick conversion if there is a bank run; in that case, the central bank will have to supply domestic currency to the banking system and base money will climb closer to broader monetary aggregates like M1 or M2.[13] Thus far, most studies that employ such ratios use M2 in the numerator; but again, this may understate potential pressures if holders of short-term government securities get nervous about the sustainability of the existing exchange rate or about the government's ability to pay. Since few countries have adequate international reserves to back broader monetary aggregates, vulnerability is going to look larger the broader the monetary aggregate chosen by the analyst. This is a judgment call.

In *sum*, the public-debt and banking indicators outlined above are only suggestive. Still, they make a point. One cannot rely exclusively either on aggregate longer term solvency indicators (e.g., total external debt to GNP) or on measures of "flow" disequilibrium (e.g., ratios of current account deficits to GNP) in gauging vulnerability. Liquidity and currency mismatches can and do occur in both public debt management and in banking systems and analysts of emerging markets should keep track of them.

A Large Current Account Deficit, Used Mainly for Consumption and Financed in Good Measure by Short-term Borrowing

When a country is running a current account deficit in its international payments, it is drawing on foreign saving to cover a shortfall in domestic saving relative to domestic investment. The current account deficit also adds to the country's stock of

---

[13] See Obstfeld and Rogoff (1995).

external debt (i.e., external debt includes the summation of all past current account deficits). The link to financial crisis typically arises when foreign investors make the judgment that the current account deficit is, for whatever reason, "unsustainably large." At that point, foreign investors will refuse to provide much further financing and the borrowing country will therefore have to "adjust"—a process that requires resort to expenditure-reducing policy (i.e., tighter monetary and fiscal policy) and/or expenditure-switching policy (usually, exchange rate devaluation). If the citizens of the borrowing country decide that the costs of adjustment (in terms of reduced economic growth and employment) are too high, they can also contribute to the crisis by encouraging the authorities to default on its external obligations. The rub of course in the current account story of financial crises is how to identify what an "unsustainably large" current account deficit is.

One perspective is to look at the *conditions for longer run equilibrium*. In the steady state, the growth of foreign debt must equal the growth of nominal income (in the debtor country). This implies that the steady-state current account deficit (as a percent of GDP) cannot exceed the rate of growth of nominal income multiplied by the maximum "safe" debt/income ratio.[14] By plugging in plausible values for these latter two variables, one can therefore derive estimates of the "safe" or "sustainable" current account deficit. A few examples (drawn from Williamson [1994]) will convey the flavor. Suppose we adopt a rule of thumb that says that the debt/income ratio cannot safely exceed 40 percent.[15] Suppose we also measure the growth of nominal income in terms of the international currency (the US dollar) in which debt is usually denominated. Then, if the trend in rate of inflation is taken

---

[14] Let D= foreign debt and Y= nominal income. $\dot{Y}/Y = \dot{D}/D$ in steady state, so $D/Y = (\dot{D}/D)(\dot{Y}/Y) = (\dot{Y}/Y)(\dot{D}/D)$.

[15] In 1994, Mexico had a ratio of external debt to GDP of 36 percent. Its ratio of gross public debt (internal plus external debt) to GDP was 57 percent—below the OECD average of 71 percent; see Sachs et al (1995). Cline (1995) argues that a threshold of 40 percent of GDP for external debt can be justified by the tendency in the historical record for countries which go beyond it to get into debt difficulties. Some analysts have preferred instead to emphasize debt/export ratios since this carries a closer link to foreign exchange availability. Here, it has been suggested that a ratio of net external debt (where net means net of foreign exchange reserves) to exports greater than 200 or 220 percent should be regarded as "unsustainable"; see Frankel and Rose (1995).

to be 3 percent (in US dollars), the steady-state current account deficit should not exceed 2.4 percent of GDP for a country with a growth rate trend of 3 percent; should not exceed 3.2 percent for a country with a growth rate trend of 5 percent; and should not exceed 5.6 percent for a country with a growth rate trend of 10 percent. If the initial debt/income ratio is low, or if the current account deficit is only temporary (say, just for a year), then these safe limits could be exceeded for a short period. But this line of argument suggests that the burden of proof should be on the borrowing country to explain why it can handle a "structural" current account deficit that exceeds 3 percent, or if it has East Asian growth rates, a structural deficit that exceeds 5 percent.

In this light, Mexico with current account deficits running 7-8 percent of GDP in 1993/94 was going beyond prudent limits. Other emerging-market economies with high average current account deficits over the 1990-1994 period include the Kingdom of Thailand (7 percent); Malaysia, Peru, and the Republic of the Philippines (5-6 percent); and Bulgaria, Chile, Romania, and Hungary (3-4.5 percent). On the other hand, the Republic of Singapore got away with running a current account deficit on the order of 10 percent of GDP for a decade. For additional perspective, one might note that the United Kingdom ran an average current account deficit equivalent to roughly 4.5 percent of GDP from 1880 to 1913, and that the Scandinavian countries were also able to maintain large average deficits over an extended period. Still, it is unusual to see a major industrial country incur a current account deficit equal to, say, 3 percent of GNP for three or more years in a row.[16] The average current account imbalance (without regard to sign) for G-7 countries over the 1980s was 1.7 percent.[17]

A potentially important adjustment that often needs to be made to observed current account positions is cyclical correction. The reason is that the current account typically deteriorates during a cyclical expansion in the borrowing country (that is not matched in its main trading partners), as imports

---

[16] For G-7 countries over the 1970-1993 period, this has happened on only three occasions: the United States, 1985-1987; the United Kingdom, 1988-1990; and Canada, 1989-1993.

[17] See Goldstein and Mussa (1994).

grow faster than exports. This suggests that a current account deficit of say, 4 percent, is likely to be more troubling if the economy is in a recession than if it is operating at full capacity. By the same token, if a country's main trading partners were expected to soon emerge from their own recessions with positive feedback effects on the home country's exports, then a 3 percent deficit might well be viewed with less concern. In short, just as one often wants to evaluate a country's fiscal position at the full employment level of output, the same kind of cyclical adjustment is warranted when assessing current account imbalances. Again, Mexico's 1994 current account deficit was rendered more serious by the fact that it was occurring against a backdrop of rather weak domestic economic growth (2 percent).

A second perspective on current account imbalances is to look at the *sources of the imbalance* or, what is often much the same thing, at how the foreign borrowing is being used. This perspective has led in the literature to a discussion of "good" and "bad" current account imbalances. For example, a current account imbalance that arises from reversible intercountry differences in the age distribution of the population—which in turn generate different life-cycle private savings patterns— is likely to be benign (so long as investors recognize the reversibility). Consumption-smoothing of clearly temporary terms of trade shock should also generate a "good" current account deficit. On the other hand, borrowing to finance a consumption binge when there is little evidence either that consumption has previously been too low or that the economy has been hit by a temporary shock would fall in the "bad" deficit camp.

Two strands in the good/bad deficit debate merit particular mention. One is the proposition that a current account deficit that primarily reflects an *increase in investment* is likely to be more sustainable than one that primarily reflects an increase in consumption. The basic idea here is that optimal foreign borrowing should proceed to the point where the (social) rate of return on that borrowing exceeds its costs, and that investment (by augmenting the country's future debt-servicing capacity and its ability to earn foreign exchange) typically stands a better chance of satisfying that condition than does consumption (unless the latter has been held at an artificially low level for a sustained period).[18] Investment-led deficits are often defended as benign in cases where is there some a priori reason to believe that domestic economic policy reforms have produced a dramatic increase in the marginal productivity of domestic investment; in such a case, one can argue that domestic investment opportunities will be ample relative to the supply of domestic saving, and that the increased capital inflow (that is the mirror image of an increased current account deficit) is temporarily financing the transition to a higher trend in growth path. In practical terms, the greater the extent of structural change in the economy, the more difficult it is likely to be to evaluate the rate of return on new investment.

Because Asian emerging market economies have channeled proportionately more of increased private capital inflows into investment than their Latin American counterparts, capital flows to the former are regarded by many observers as more sustainable than those to the latter.[19] It has also been noticed that while Mexico's current account deficit (as a share of GDP) increased by 6.6 percentage points between 1989 and 1993, its investment share (again relative to GDP) rose by only 0.7 percentage point;[20] moreover, capital goods represented only a minor share of Mexico's total imports.[21]

Figure 6.6, adapted from Artus et al (1995), provides a capsule summary of the size of current account imbalances and investment shares for a group of emerging market economies. On the argument that investment-led current account deficits are less cause for concern than consumption-led ones of commensurate size, the more vulnerable countries would be those in the southwest quadrant, that is, those with relatively large current account

---

[18] An illustration of the point that consumption-led current account deficits are not always maligned is the Romanian experience. In the late 1980s, the Ceaucescu regime manipulated the saving-investment balance to ensure current account surpluses so that the entire external debt could be repaid. As a result, there was a sharp decline in living standards, in the quality of investment, and in economic growth; see Calvo et al (1996). Here, an increase in consumption could justifiably be regarded as a move toward a more sustainable level.

[19] See Calvo et al (1994) and Leiderman and Thorne (1996).

[20] See Leiderman and Thorne (1996).

[21] See Fischer (1994).

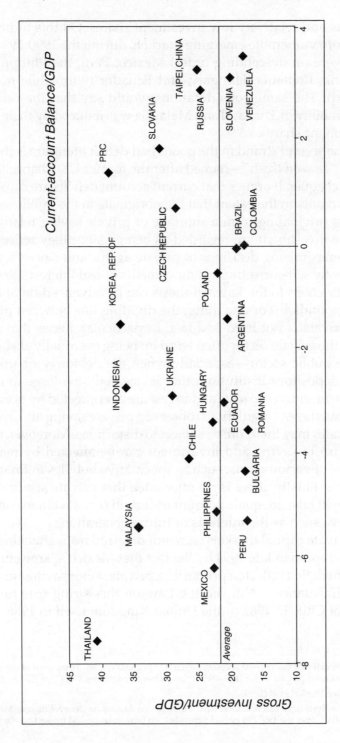

Figure 6.6   Gross Investment and Current Account Balance as Percent of GDP, 1990-1994 Average

Source: Artus et al (1995).

deficits and relatively low investment shares. On this indicator, the more vulnerable emerging markets during the 1990-1994 period were (in descending order) Mexico, Peru, the Philippines, Bulgaria, Romania, Hungary, and Ecuador (with Chile not far behind). The same considerations would say that the relative vulnerability of Thailand and Malaysia was reduced by their high investment shares.

The second strand in the good/bad deficit literature is the so-called "*Lawson thesis*"—named after the former UK Chancellor of the Exchequer. It argues that current account deficits are cause for concern only to the extent that they originate in the public sector; deficits originating from a shortage of private saving relative to private investment are regarded as benign since they reflect the profit-maximizing decisions of private agents and since they are inherently self-correcting via movements in real interest rates.[22]

Objections to the Lawson thesis can be advanced on at least four grounds.[23] For one thing, the dividing line between public and private is not hard-and-fast. In particular, losses that start out in the private sector often wind up being eventually absorbed by the public sector—especially when the debtor is a bank (or other depository institution) that is deemed "too large to fail." Private incentives to save and invest are also affected by tax rates and government regulations; observed private saving and investment rates may therefore be subject to distortions. Moreover, rates of return to saving and investment can be affected by market failures of various sorts, such as speculative bubbles in financial markets. Finally, there is no guarantee that private sector decisions will take adequate account of certain social welfare considerations, such as the interests of future generations.

Private capital markets were not deterred from attacking the Mexican peso in late 1994 by the fact that Mexico's large current account deficit reflected primarily a private sector saving/investment imbalance.[24] Nor did the Lawson thesis ring true for the cases of Chile in 1981 or the United Kingdom itself in 1986.

---

[22] Recall that the current account deficit (CA) can be written as the sum of the public sector (G-T) and private sector (I-S) saving/investment imbalances; i.e., CA = (G-T) + (I-S).

[23] See Frenkel et al (1991).

[24] Analysts have reached somewhat different conclusions on the evolution of Mexico's fiscal position over the 1993/94 period depending on how inflation and interest on the public

To *sum up*, one should always try to examine the source of a current account imbalance before making judgments about its sustainability. In addition, the sustainable current account deficit is likely to differ across countries. That being said, there are good reasons for analysts to be wary about a current account deficit that exceeds 4-5 percent of GDP—especially if the deficit is persistent, primarily reflects an increase in consumption, occurs while the economy is operating well below its level of potential output, and is financed in significant part by short-term portfolio flows. Even though current account deficits only represent additions to the stock of external debt, capital markets are likely to view these changes in terms of their sustainability over the longer term. And if corrective action (or another source of reversibility) is not seen as on the near horizon, an unsustainable debt/reserve position in the future can lead markets to take defensive action immediately—thereby precipitating the crisis.

A Highly Overvalued Real Exchange Rate, Exacerbated by "Politicization" of Exchange Rate Decisions

If market participants expect a large, near-term depreciation/ devaluation of the current exchange rate (beyond that implied by nominal interest rate differentials), they will have very considerable incentives either to get out of unhedged long positions in the domestic currency (so as to avoid a capital loss), or to "short" the domestic currency (so as to profit from its decline).[25] The longer the overvaluation continues, the greater the likelihood both that market pressures will build and that the country's ability to defend the disequilibrium rate will erode (as larger current account deficits drain the country's reserves).

The ERM crises in the fall of 1992 and the summer of 1993, and the Mexican crisis of late 1994 provide vivid illustrations of overvalued (fixed or quasi-fixed) exchange rates coming to dis-

---

debt are treated in the measurement of the public sector imbalance, and on whether lending through development banks is treated as part of the fiscal deficit; see Leiderman and Thorne (1996) and Sachs et al (1995). Nevertheless, the conclusion that the current account deficit was predominantly a private sector saving/investment imbalance is not debatable.

[25] As noted by Eichengreen (1995), a 10 percent devaluation expected to occur in 10 days with a probability of 90 percent offers risk-neutral investors an expected annualized return of nearly 500 percent.

orderly, market-forced corrections. In these cases, the exchange rate correction could have taken place earlier—by a smaller amount and in a less chaotic fashion, if the authorities in the devaluing country(ies) had agreed to accept a devaluation. They did not— in part because devaluation was seen as having unfavorable political costs; as such, there was a tendency to delay.

One tack toward getting an early warning of an impending currency crisis is to focus on the *discrepancy between the actual real exchange rate and the equilibrium real exchange rate*; the larger this so-called "misalignment" is, the greater the likelihood of a crisis. This requires the analyst to identify the equilibrium real exchange rate. By now, there is extensive literature on the various techniques available for estimating (real) equilibrium exchange rates for both industrial and developing countries.[26] It is sufficient here to outline two relevant possibilities.[27]

One long-standing approach is to use *purchasing-power parity* (PPP) to estimate the equilibrium exchange rate.[28] In brief, if one can identify a base period in which the country was (approximately) in external balance, then the equilibrium value of the nominal exchange rate in the current period is the base-period value adjusted for the (cumulative) intercountry difference in inflation rates between the current and base periods; that is, it is the nominal exchange rate that would restore the *real* exchange rate of the base period.

The advantage of PPP is its ease of calculation. But arrayed against that are at least three serious weaknesses and/or practical problems. The most serious one is that (contrary to the

[26] See Williamson (1994) and Clark et al (1994). These approaches apply to both fixed and floating exchange rate regimes because the real equilibrium exchange rate (i.e., the nominal exchange rate deflated by inflation differences across the two countries) can be defined equally well under either regime.

[27] A third possibility would be to look at the "black market" (parallel market) rate for guidance as to the equilibrium rate. The rub is that the black market may be too thin to offer a reliable estimate. Portes (1991), for example, argues that the black market rate will only reflect the prices of a few acutely scarce goods, and that it is likely to undervalue the currency not only with respect to purchasing power parity, but also to any other plausible equilibrium concept. Still, the black market premium may offer some hint as to the order of magnitude of misalignment. Edwards (1994) uses the parallel-market premium as one of the explanatory variables for the time-series behavior of real exchange rates in a sample of 12 developing countries.

[28] There are both absolute and relative versions of PPP. The absolute version says that the equilibrium exchange rate between two currencies is the one that equates purchasing power in those currencies. The relative version is outlined above.

assumption of PPP) the equilibrium real exchange rate will normally change over time, reflecting, inter alia, permanent changes in the terms of trade, changes in debtor-creditor positions, and changes in productivity growth. For example, a country that was a small international debtor in the base period will not have the same equilibrium real exchange rate if it is a large international debtor in the current period. Similarly, it is well documented that countries with unusually high productivity growth in tradable goods relative to that in nontradables (typically, relatively fast growing countries) will experience a rise in the relative price of nontradables (vis-à-vis tradable goods).[29] This, in turn, will cause a PPP-based measure of the real exchange rate, computed using consumer price indices, to show trend appreciation. If no correction is made for this productivity bias, PPP calculations will produce a misleading estimate of the equilibrium exchange rate. An additional problem is that it is often not easy to identify an equilibrium base period. And third, empirical research suggests that PPP does not provide a good explanation of actual exchange rate behavior, except over the very long term (decades), or under conditions of hyperinflation, or when the price basket is restricted to a rather narrow set of goods (homogeneous primary commodities); as such, it may not be so helpful in gauging equilibrium rates over, say, two-four year periods when the countries in question have moderate inflation differences. Still, if real exchange rates have changed (particularly, appreciated) by a great deal over a relatively short period, questions should be asked as to what change in fundamentals could have justified such a change in the equilibrium rate.

A second way to go—with a much firmer grounding—is to define the equilibrium rate as the real exchange rate that will permit simultaneous attainment of both internal and external balance. By internal balance, one means that the economy is operating either at full capacity output or at its noninflationary unemployment rate (its NAIRU). External balance is typically defined as a situation where the current account imbalance can be sustainably financed by "normal" capital flows.

---

[29] This is known in the literature as the "productivity-bias" hypothesis or the "Balassa-Samuelson effect."

A key advantage of this "underlying balance" approach is that it both permits the equilibrium exchange rate to change over time and integrates the exchange rate with the more ultimate objectives of economic policy. A practical problem for application to emerging-market economies is that the estimation of the equilibrium rate is more time-consuming and complicated.

The chief conceptual problem lies with the notion of "normal" capital flows. This is simply the other side of the coin of gauging a sustainable current account. While extreme values of current account imbalances (say, 8-10 percent of GDP or more) are not difficult to rule out of bounds, it is apt to be much harder to defend why, say, a zero current account balance is to be preferred to, say, a 2 percent deficit. In other words, there can be a range of current account imbalances over which there is no convincing unique value for the equilibrium exchange rate.[30] This implies that the technique will be more useful for identifying large misalignments than small ones.

Another problem in the emerging market context is how to identify the level of potential output (or the NAIRU). Here, one will not have available the estimates of potential output—and of output gaps—that are now commonplace for major industrial countries. Judgments about the desirable feedback effects of exchange rate changes on internal balance may therefore have to be made on more approximate criteria (e.g., a devaluation would help to raise the now anemic growth rate to a more satisfactory range).

A related practical problem for the emerging market analyst is that unless a macroeconomic model is available for the country in question, it will not be possible to "solve" for the equilibrium real exchange rate that would simultaneously deliver the "desired" or "equilibrium" values of internal and external balance. Again, what is now routinely available for major industrial countries may not be for most emerging market economies.

Still, compromises that are possible should convey useful hints to the analyst. On the modeling side, several researchers

---

[30] This in turn reflects the view that there is a range of values for the ratio of external debt/GNP that are "sustainable."

(e.g., Edwards [1994] and Elbadawi [1994]) have recently formulated small empirical models of real exchange rates for a set of developing countries that permit one to derive estimates of misalignment. In these models, the equilibrium real exchange rate is defined as the relative price of nontradables and tradables; the "fundamentals" driving real equilibrium exchange rates are proxied by observable variables such as the terms of trade, the degree of trade openness, and the share of government consumption in GNP; other variables (like the rate of domestic credit expansion) are allowed to produce temporary changes in the real exchange rate; and mechanisms are specified for how departures from the equilibrium real exchange rate are corrected over time. At a more basic level, even if no econometric model of the economy or the real exchange rate is available, the basic insight of the underlying balance approach can still be applied. Specifically, the analyst should ask: what are reasonable longer term current account and domestic growth targets for the country in question; is the existing level of the real exchange rate likely to be (remotely) consistent with the achievement of these targets; and if not, in what direction—and by what rough order of magnitude—would the real exchange rate of this country have to move to get close to these targets? Even a back-of-the-envelope calculation might do some good in spotting large (say, 20 percent or larger) misalignments.

Instead of looking at misalignments, one might try to foresee currency crises by looking at *market indicators of expected exchange rate changes*; the most accessible one is the exchange rate change implied by interest rate differentials on otherwise comparable securities that are denominated in different currencies. These market indicators can be used in two ways. First, for countries with publicly announced exchange rate targets, one can ask whether market indicators of expected exchange rate changes are consistent with the government's announced exchange rate targets.[31] If the market's expectation falls outside the announced range, one can regard the official target as less than credible—with the presumption that the market will soon force a change

---

[31] See Svensson (1991). Of course, there is also the possibility that the market's expectation about the equilibrium exchange rate is unreasonable; see the later discussion.

in the official parity or zone. One can also view a sharp widening of the interest rate spreads as indicative of increased market concerns about currency risk. Second, for countries that maintain floating rates, one can ask whether the market's current forecast seems to be sustainable and, if not, in which direction it is likely to move. Let me elaborate.

Abstracting from the presence of a risk premium, the notion of uncovered interest rate parity says that (with open capital markets) the interest rate differential between two otherwise identical securities that differ only with respect to the currency of denomination should be equal to the expected change in the exchange rate between those two currencies. For example, if market participants expect the peso to depreciate vis-à-vis the US dollar by 20 percent between now and the end of the year, then (arbitrage will dictate that) one-year peso-denominated securities have to pay an interest rate 20 percent higher than dollar-denominated ones. Of course, if the two securities differ in other respects (e.g., liquidity, tax treatment, default risk, etc.), then the observed interest rate differential will reflect a combination of these factors plus currency risk, and the comparison will be less useful for the purpose at hand; nevertheless, if these other differences remain roughly constant over time, then a widening of the differential might still convey some useful information about changes over time in expected exchange rate changes.

In the case of the Mexican crisis, the predictive performance of interest rate differentials was mixed. Figure 6.7 looks at the interest rate differential between one-year *cetes* and one-year *tesobonos* and compares the implied market expectation of peso movements with the maximum one-year depreciation rate under Mexico's announced crawling peg. Figure 6.7 suggests that after the Colosio assassination in March 1994, the market's expectation of peso depreciation was fairly consistent beyond the rate promised by the authorities—implying that the government's exchange rate objective was not fully credible. As suggested by Obstfeld and Rogoff (1995), reading the tea leaves here is not straightforward because the interest rate differential might also be signaling differential default risk on the two securities; in addition, the gap between the market and official exchange rates is widest in the summer of 1994 when the attack occurred with most ferocity only in late

**Figure 6.7   Mexico: Interest Rate Differentials and the
Exchange Rate Band, Weekly Data,
July 1993-December 1994**

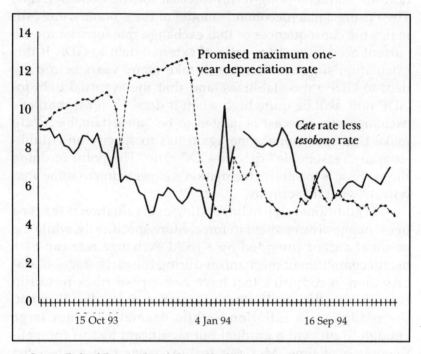

Source: Federal Reserve Board. From Obstfeld and Rogoff (1995).

December.[32] It is likewise interesting to note that interest rate differentials showed no strong indication of impending currency crises prior to the ERM crises of 1992/93.[33] In short, interest rate differentials sometimes provide a good clue about coming exchange market pressures, and sometimes not. Nevertheless, because they sometimes provide very useful information, they are definitely worth monitoring.

Assessing whether the market's current forecast for a particular currency is itself a reasonable one requires an exercise

---

[32] Indicators of default risk on *tesobonos* jumped up sharply in April 1994 but stayed roughly constant between then and the outbreak of the crisis; see Calvo and Goldstein (1996).

[33] See Rose and Svensson (1994).

that harks back to our earlier discussion of sustainable current accounts. Here, one again uses interest rate differentials (usually on longer term securities if they are available) to obtain the market's (long-term) forecast for the exchange rate. Then using a macroeconomic model of the economy, one estimates the consequences of that exchange rate forecast for the current account and the ratio of external debt to GDP. If this calculation suggests that it will take many years before the debt-to-GDP ratio stabilizes, and that the eventual debt-to-GDP ratio will be quite high when it does, then the market's exchange rate forecast is judged to be "unsustainable."[34] To make this operational, one again has to specify an equilibrium or "reasonable" debt-to-GDP ratio. The point of doing the exercise is to subject the market's expectation to some analytical "what if" scrutiny.

An additional clue to impending overvaluation is the type of exchange arrangement in force. More specifically, while the nominal anchor provided by a fixed exchange rate can be a useful commitment mechanism during the early stages of stabilization in countries that have had a poor track record in controlling inflation via other approaches, more often than not, the reduction in inflation—while dramatic—is not large enough to prevent a gradual but significant loss in competitiveness over time. Mexico's real exchange rate appreciated by about 30 percent between 1989 and the outbreak of the crisis.[35] Figure 6.8 shows a similar pattern of real exchange rate appreciation for four ERM countries (Italy, Portugal, Spain, and Sweden) prior to the 1992/93 crisis. The nominal anchor role of a fixed exchange rate can overstay its welcome. At some point, a shift to greater exchange rate flexibility of one sort or another will be needed to address a loss of competitiveness— before the misalignment gets so large as to generate a crisis-driven devaluation. Analysts ought to beware of this poten-

---

[34] This kind of "sustainability" exercise was employed by Marris (1985) and Krugman (1985) to argue that the market's then forecast for the US dollar implied unsustainable debt dynamics and would therefore have to be substantially revised.

[35] This calculation uses consumer prices to deflate the nominal exchange rate. The appreciation of the real exchange rate over this period is significantly smaller if one uses wholesale prices instead; see Sachs et al (1995).

Figure 6.8 Real Exchange Rates Against the Deutsche Mark for Four European Countries

A. Italy: real lira/DM exchange rate
Quarterly data, 1987:1-1994:1

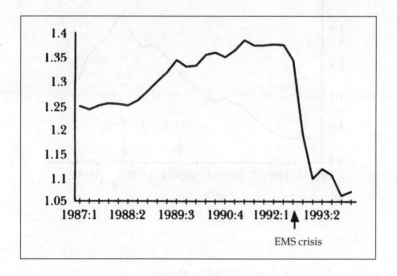

B. Spain: real peseta/DM exchange rate
Quarterly data, 1987:1-1994:2

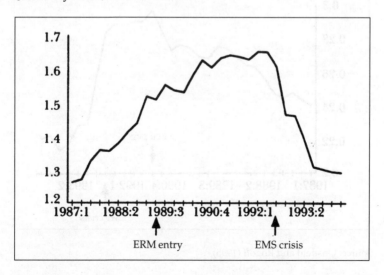

Figure 6.8 (continued)

C. Portugal: real escudo/DM exchange rate
Quarterly data, 1987:1-1994:2

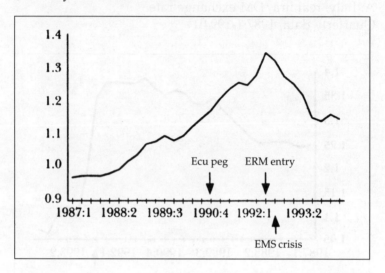

D. Sweden: real krona/DM exchange rate
Quarterly data, 1987:1-1994:2

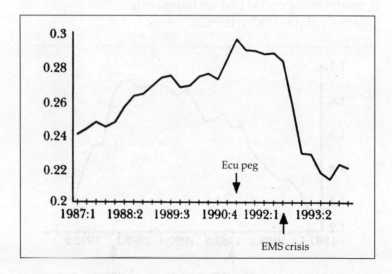

Source: Obstfeld and Rogoff (1995).

tial problem for countries that are operating under fixed or quasi-fixed exchange arrangements.

Yet a final element that ought to be brought into the picture is the degree of "politicization" of exchange rate decisions. With the benefit of hindsight, there is little doubt that the decision to delay a devaluation of the Mexico peso was heavily influenced by the upcoming presidential election. Similarly, even though the need for a revaluation of the deutsche mark was apparent in 1991 and early 1992, Germany's ERM partners apparently did not want to suffer the political embarrassment of presiding over a devaluation; as such, they attempted to "hold on" to existing parities for too long. All these suggest that vulnerability to currency crisis will be increased when sitting authorities place particularly heavy political costs on a devaluation (since this will increase the probability of delay).

To *sum up*, even though the identification and estimation of exchange rate misalignment in emerging markets is sure to be subject to a considerable margin of uncertainty/error, the analyst ought to be monitoring closely the evolution of the real exchange rate. In cases where the existing real exchange rate has undergone a sizeable appreciation relative to trend, and/or where the economy is both generating a large current account deficit and experiencing slow growth (or a recession), and/or where interest differentials point to increasing currency risk, a yellow light should be flashing as to the possibility of a currency crisis.[36] Moreover, there is increasing evidence that large overvaluation of the real exchange rate also provides a good early warning of banking crises, reflecting, among other things, the effect of overvaluation on the creditworthiness of exporters and on the buildup of currency mismatches by banks and their customers.[37]

---

[36] Where a country is maintaining a fixed exchange rate, another potential clue for a currency crisis—stressed in the early literature on speculative attacks (Krugman [1979])—is an expansion of domestic credit beyond the demand for money, often driven in turn by a large fiscal deficit.

[37] See Goldstein and Turner (1996) and Kaminsky and Reinhart (1996).

Constraints (Most of Which Relate to Financial Fragility) on the Willingness to Increase Domestic Interest Rates When There Is a Sharp Drop-off in Capital Inflows Or a Speculative Attack on the Domestic Currency

Aside from the exchange rate, the other key variable that acts as an equilibrating mechanism for shifts in international capital flows is the interest rate. When capital is moving out of a country and/or its exchange rate is under strong downward pressure, an increase in the domestic interest rate serves two purposes: it makes assets denominated in the domestic currency more attractive (at the margin), and it makes it more expensive for speculators to "short" the domestic currency (by making them pay more to acquire the domestic currency needed to fulfill their forward contracts). Yet we often observe that countries under pressure are reluctant to undertake (or to sustain) those sharp increases in domestic interest rates that might forestall, or lessen the duration of, a crisis. Why so?

The most convincing answer is *financial fragility* of one type or another. When such fragility is present, the increase in domestic interest rates will simply be too costly or too unpopular to undertake or to sustain; it may even exacerbate the crisis. Three specific kinds of fragility merit explicit mention.

One is *weaknesses in the domestic banking system.* An increase in interest rates typically has a contractionary effect on the economy that increases loan delinquencies. The same interest rate increase will also depress asset prices—including real estate prices; since real estate and equities often constitute the collateral for loans, this too will undermine the value of the bank's loan book. Banks' funding costs and income position could likewise be adversely affected.[38] If the banking system already is laboring under a relatively high ratio of nonperforming loans to total loans, authorities may worry that a large increase in domestic interest rates would push banks "over the edge." In this connection, the reluctance of the Mexican authorities to increase domestic interest rates in the spring of 1994 surely owed much

---

[38] Other financial firms that use short-term rollover credits to fund trading positions can also be put in jeopardy by a sharp, unexpected increase in interest rates.

to the fact that the ratio of nonperforming loans to total loans at Mexican banks had climbed from over 4 percent in early 1991 to over 8 percent in mid-1994. The same considerations about the health of the domestic banking system also help to explain why Sweden found it impossible to sustain a 500 percent marginal lending rate in September 1992, and in contrast, why the Hong Kong authorities were able to implement a significant increase in domestic interest rates (in the immediate aftermath of the Mexican crisis) to squash a run on the Hong Kong dollar.[39]

A second source of fragility can be a weak government fiscal position, characterized by a *large fiscal deficit, with a high proportion of short-term debt carrying floating interest rates*. In that situation, a sharp increase in domestic interest rates can feedback quickly to increase substantially the government's funding costs and to undermine confidence in the authorities' ability to manage the crisis. The classic example of this constraint limiting the room for interest rate action was Italy's situation during the ERM crisis.

As with exchange rate policy, *political considerations* also matter. In this respect, two other factors limit the scope for an aggressive interest rate defense. A high unemployment rate is one of them—particularly if it is paired with slow growth and relatively low inflation. In that circumstance, the public will put a high internal opportunity cost on orienting interest rate policy to external concerns. The incidence of the interest rate increase is the other factor. If it is known that an increase in short-term rates would feed quickly through the yield curve (affecting mortgage rates and the like) and, in so doing, work to alienate a good part (e.g., homeowners) of the governing party's electoral support, the authorities (especially if the central bank has relatively low independence) may find the prospect sufficiently unappetizing as to avoid it. The facts that the United Kingdom had already suffered seven consecutive quarters of recession prior to the ERM crisis and that short-term interest rates there feed quickly through to mortgage rates, are often cited as having limited the UK authorities room for maneuver.[40]

---

[39] See IMF (1995).
[40] See Goldstein et al (1993a).

In *sum*, when gauging an emerging market's vulnerability to either a reversal in capital flows or a speculative attack on a fixed exchange rate, a good question to ask is the following: as part of its policy response, would the country be able (on financial fragility and political grounds) to sharply increase domestic interest rates and to hold them there long enough to defuse market pressures? Countries with already beleaguered banking systems, weak fiscal positions, high unemployment, slow growth rates, and unpopular governments are going to be handicapped in mounting such an interest rate defense—and speculators know it and presumably take it into account in deciding which are the candidates most susceptible to a successful attack. Analysts need to do the same calculus.

A Boom in Bank Lending, Followed by a Sharp Decline in Asset Prices

Not only have banking crises been a prominent feature of the financial landscape in both industrial and developing countries over the last two decades, but also the public sector cost of resolving those crises has been huge. Indeed, Table 6.1, taken from Caprio and Klingebiel (1996), shows that there have been a dozen episodes where the public resolution of banking crises has been equal to 10 percent of GDP or more. Honohan (1996) estimates that the total bailout costs of banking crises in all developing countries since 1980 have approached US$250 billion.[41]

There has long been a school of thought (Kindleberger [1978]) that sees financial crises as being promoted by excessive credit creation and unsound finance during the expansion phase of the business cycle, only to come crashing down when the bubble inevitably bursts. The upswing begins with an exogenous event that justifies an increase in asset prices. The building of the bubble is then reinforced by higher leverage, a move by banks to shorten the maturity structure of their liabilities relative to assets, the effect of higher prices on the real value of debt, and the positive

---

[41] For a fuller discussion of the costs of developing-country banking crises, including potential spillover effects on industrial countries, see Goldstein and Turner (1996) and Goldstein (1997).

Table 6.1   Severe Banking Crises, 1980-1996

Country (time period)	Estimate of Total Losses/Costs (percent of GDP)
Central and Latin America	
Argentina (1980-1982)	55
Chile (1981-1983)	41[a]
Venezuela (1994-1995)	18
Mexico (1995)	12-15[b]
Africa	
Benin (1988-1990)	17
Cote d'Ivoire (1988-1991)	25
Mauritania (1984-1993)	15
Senegal (1988-1991)	17
Tanzania (1987-1995)	10[c]
Middle East	
Israel (1977-1983)	30[d]
Transition Economies of Eastern Europe	
Bulgaria (1990s)	14
Hungary (1995)	10
Industrial Countries	
Spain (1977-1985)	17
Japan (1990s)	10[e]

[a] 1982 -1985
[b] Accumulated losses.
[c] In 1987.
[d] In 1983.
[e] Estimate of potential losses.

Source: Caprio and Klingebiel (1996).

feedback provided by early profits. Eventually, the bubble bursts when a negative exogenous shock (e.g., a stock market crash, a large dip in the terms of trade, a recession abroad, etc.) causes investors to lose confidence and run for the exits.

Recently, several authors employed a similar story to identify bank lending booms as a leading indicator of banking crises, especially in emerging market economies.[42] They argue that when the banking system as a whole is expanding rapidly, bankers find it particularly difficult to sort out bad risks from good ones. During periods of macroeconomic expansion, borrowers are transitorily very profitable and liquid. Even lower quality borrowers therefore have little trouble in passing liquidity tests for solvency (since when credit is plentiful, borrowers can easily obtain credit from other lenders). Also, when loan portfolios are expanding rapidly, their riskiness increases because banks extend credit to new customers about whom they have less information on creditworthiness. The value of loan collateral (often real estate) is also rising during expansions, making loans seem safer (even though in reality the value of that collateral is heavily influenced by the same factors affecting the borrower's ability to pay).

Figure 6.9 confirms that some notable banking crises have in fact been preceded by a very rapid growth in banking system credit measured as a proportion to GDP.[43] Case studies of banking crises/problems in both emerging markets and industrial countries likewise testify to the important role often played by sharp declines in equity and real estate prices (often coinciding with the onset of recession).[44] These asset price declines figure prominently in banking crises because of high loan concentration in these sectors, because increased speculation by banks in securities markets has sometimes followed financial liberalization, because declines in these asset prices lower the value of collateral underlying loans, and because the reduction in net worth accompanying a large de-

---

[42] See Gavin and Hausman (1995).

[43] I say "some" banking crises because several studies (e.g., Caprio and Klingebiel [1996] and Kaminsky and Reinhart [1996]) suggest that lending booms do not perform quite as well as some other leading indicators of banking crises when the sample is extended to a larger group of developing countries.

[44] See Balino and Sundararajan (1991), Caprio et al (1994), Goldstein et al (1993b), and Kaminsky and Reinhart (1996).

Figure 6.9   Bank Lending Booms and Banking Crises

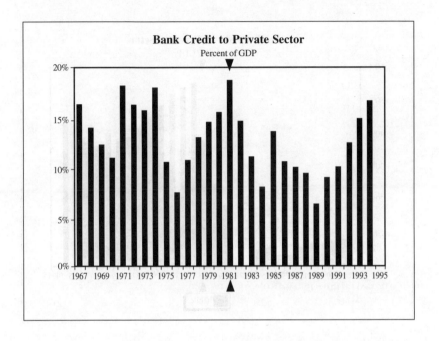

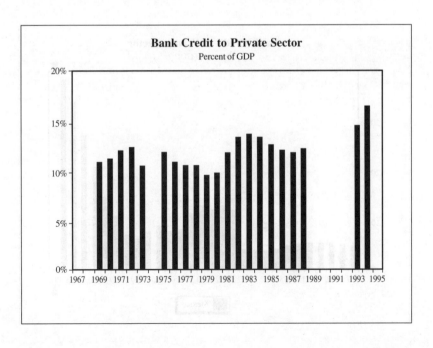

Figure 6.9   (continued)

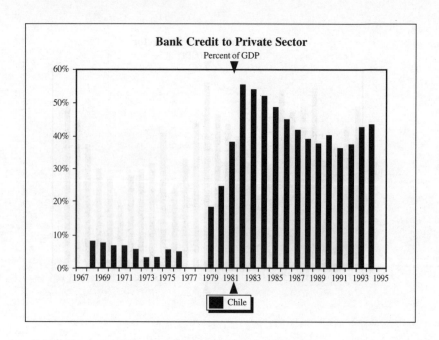

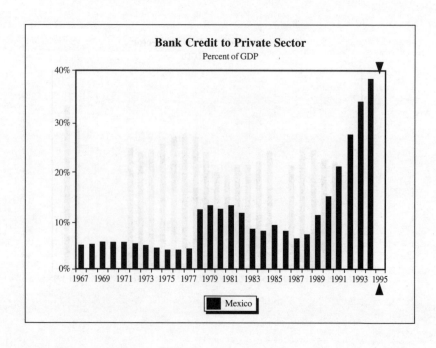

Figure 6.9   (continued)

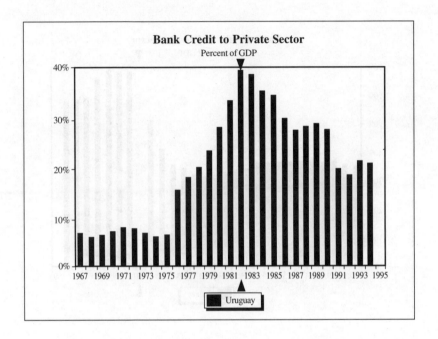

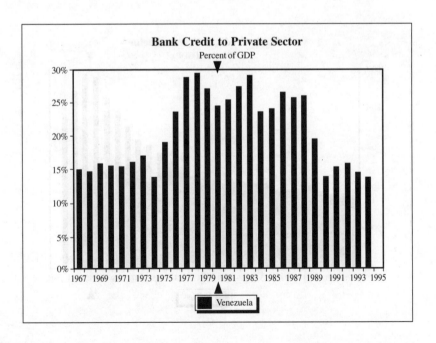

Figure 6.9 (continued)

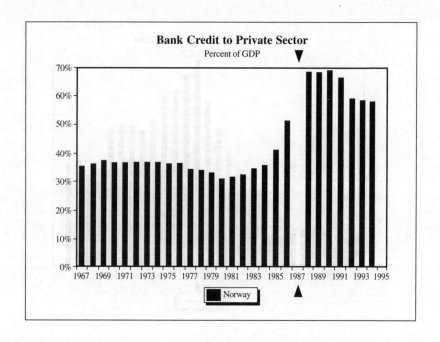

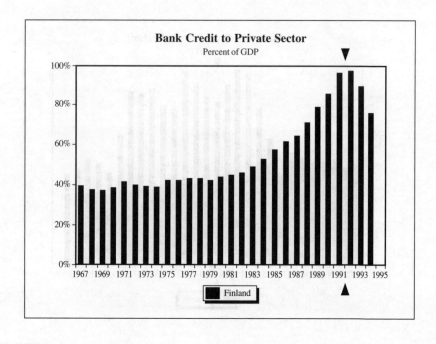

Figure 6.9   (continued)

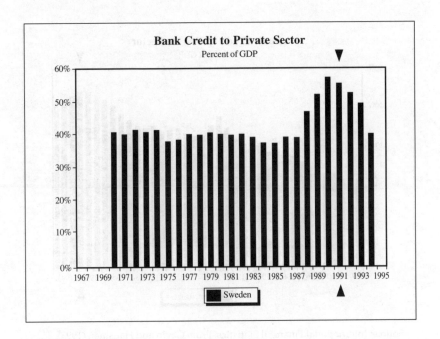

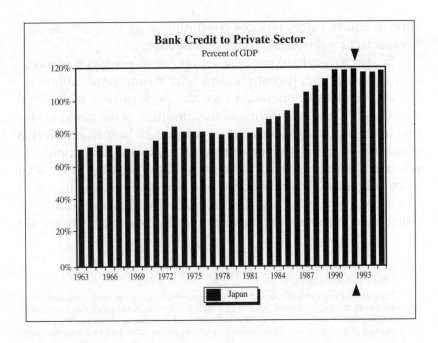

Figure 6.9 (continued)

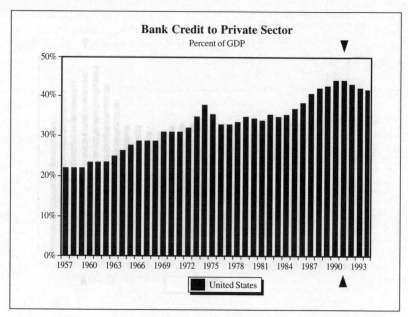

Source: International Financial Statistics. From Gavin and Hausman (1995).

cline in equity prices reduces consumption and exacerbates adverse selection problems in credit markets.

In *sum*, when banking crises do occur in emerging markets, they can be extremely costly affairs, with serious implications, inter alia, for fiscal deficits and for the performance of the real economy.[45] Close monitoring of the condition of the banking system in these countries is therefore warranted. In such an effort, a rapid run-up in banking-system credit relative to GDP should be taken as a warning signal. So too should the bursting of an asset price bubble (particularly, equity and real estate prices), the onset of a recession, and a sharp rise in domestic real interest rates.[46] A rising trend in the ratio of nonperforming loans to total loans should

---

[45] See Goldstein '(1997).

[46] It might be argued that it would be even better to have early warning of banking crises *before* the asset price bubble bursts. Yes, but that itself may be difficult to predict and econometric work (Kaminsky and Reinhart [1996]) indicates that a declining stock market provides early warning of banking crises. In developing countries where bank stocks are actively traded

likewise initiate increased attention (although its usefulness is admittedly often blunted by the practice of "evergreening" bad loans).[47] On the qualitative side, any emerging market economy that has allowed the pace of financial liberalization to proceed much faster than the strengthening of banking supervision—especially when banking supervision is subject to strong political pressures—should be included in the likely list of future banking trouble spots.[48] Finally, given the all too frequent practice of using the banking system as a vehicle for channeling government assistance (off-budget) to ailing industries, and the extremely poor track record of state-owned banks, analysts should take a close look at banking systems where government involvement/government ownership is relatively high.[49]

High Susceptibility to "Contagion" After Onset of Financial Crises Elsewhere

The Mexican crisis put the spotlight on the contagion of financial difficulties among developing countries. A diverse group of emerging markets in both Latin America and Asia experienced (downward) pressure in their equity, bond, or foreign exchange markets in the immediate aftermath of the Mexican crisis.[50] The US$64,000 question is what determines the country pattern of such "contagion"? Answering that question for emerging markets is difficult because there are multiple sources of contagion and because the empirical evidence for distinguishing among them is still relatively limited.

The literature mentions at least three potential sources of contagion.[51] One is the traditional linkage via *bilateral trade and*

---

and not subject to serious manipulation, there may also be some mileage in the behavior of bank stocks (relative, say, to their book value or to the behavior of broader equity price indices in the country); I am not aware, however, of tests of this proposition in emerging markets.

[47] See Goldstein (1997).

[48] In addition to observing the dismantling of restrictions themselves, some studies have shown that financial liberalization in developing countries is typically accompanied, inter alia, by a rise in the money multiplier and an increase in real interest rates; see Kaminsky and Reinhart (1996).

[49] See Goldstein and Turner (1996) for figures on government ownership in the banking system (as a share of total banking assets) in a group of developing countries.

[50] See IMF (1995).

[51] See Calvo and Reinhart (1996).

capital market flows. For example, if Venezuela relies more on Mexico for its exports than does Costa Rica, one would expect, ceteris paribus, a financial crisis in Mexico to have a larger adverse effect on Venezuela's creditworthiness than on Costa Rica's. Similarly, if Mexican banks have stronger and more extensive ties with banks in Argentina than with those in Colombia, then a Mexican banking crisis would be transmitted with greater force, ceteris paribus, to the former than to the latter.

A second source of contagion is *interdependencies in creditors' portfolios.* If, as a result of the Mexican crisis, an open-end emerging market mutual fund expects an increase in redemptions, it may have to sell off its equity holdings in other emerging markets to obtain liquidity. Likewise, a macro hedge fund that operates in a number of markets and that suffers, say, large losses on its bond position may have to close out some of its open positions in other markets (currencies, equities, etc.) in order to meet internal risk-control guidelines.

Third and finally, there is the so-called *herd behavior* on the part of creditors. This could occur for either rational or irrational reasons (although it is usually taken to indicate the latter). Creditors could, for example, regard the failure of one large emerging market borrower as a signal that their previous credit evaluation of all relatively high-risk borrowers was inappropriate and, on the basis of a reevaluation of fundamentals, demand higher (albeit not identical) risk premiums from all emerging market borrowers. Or creditors may find it difficult in the short run to gauge which countries are most affected by a crisis elsewhere and "flee to quality" while they sort out those spillovers (alternatively, the flight to quality may reflect the judgment that information and incentive compatibility problems typically worsen during a crisis and that low-quality borrowers are most prone to those problems).[52] Less generously, capital markets may simply suffer from "bandwagon effects" where creditors do not discriminate among borrowers on the basis of fundamentals after the onset of a crisis.

At this point, the empirical evidence on "contagion" of financial disturbances suggests the following conclusions. First, contagion is greater during periods of turbulence than during more tran-

---

[52] Mishkin (1994), for example, favors the latter interpretation.

quil times.[53] In this connection, correlation of returns on Brady bonds as between Mexico and three other large emerging markets in Latin America was much higher during the crisis period (mid-December 1994 to March 1995) than during either 1993 or 1994.[54] Similarly, cross-country correlations on weekly stock returns in emerging markets increased during the crisis period.[55] Second (and not surprisingly), the dominant direction of contagion runs from large countries to smaller ones. This means from industrial countries to emerging markets, and within emerging markets, from larger ones (like Mexico) to smaller ones.[56] Third, contagion across emerging markets seems to operate more on "regional" than on "global" lines, with most spillovers from the Mexican crisis taking place in Latin America rather than in Asia. Fourth, many financial crises are indeed characterized by a "flight to quality" in which the spread on bonds between high- and low-quality borrowers rises sharply.[57]

And fifth, the jury is still out on the extent of contagion in emerging markets that goes beyond induced movements in fundamentals (i.e., herding behavior); that said, the evidence is stronger for such contagion in the short run than in the long run.[58] In this context, a recent IMF (1995) report documents that once the initial reactions subsided, it was countries with characteristics relatively similar to Mexico's (i.e., a large current account deficit, a weak banking system, a low saving rate, and a high share of short-term debt) that were the hardest hit (i.e., Argentina and, to a lesser extent, Brazil in Latin America, and the Philippines, and to some extent, the Republic of Indonesia within Asia). At the same time, predicting contagion on the basis of any single characteristic didn't fare too well. As noted by Calvo and Reinhart (1996), Colombia, Malaysia, and Thailand each shared large current account deficits with Mexico but were not much affected by the Mexican crisis, while Brazil, which

---

[53] See Goldstein and Mussa (1994).

[54] See IMF (1995).

[55] See Calvo and Reinhart (1996).

[56] Calvo and Reinhart (1996) show that there was contagion after the Mexican crisis from six relatively large, emerging market economies (Argentina, Brazil, Chile, Colombia, Mexico, and Peru) to four relatively small ones (Costa Rica, Ecuador, El Salvador, and Uruguay)—but not in the opposite direction. There was also probably some contagion in the Mexican crisis from Mexico to some other large emerging markets; see IMF (1995).

[57] See Mishkin (1994).

[58] See Calvo and Reinhart (1996) for a review of this evidence.

then had a rather modest current account deficit, was subject to considerable turbulence. Also, Chile and Colombia weathered the crisis relatively well despite experiencing rather sharp real exchange rate appreciations in recent years. Calvo and Reinhart (1996) regard lack of an established track record in sound economic management and a rich history of failed stabilizations as perhaps the most convincing common thread. In the short term, some economies with quite strong fundamentals (e.g., Hong Kong, Malaysia, and Singapore) came under market pressure after the Mexican crisis. Why? We don't know.

In sum, almost all indicators suggest that developing countries' capital markets are now more integrated with global capital markets than they were two or three decades ago. While this increased integration offers emerging markets potentially significant benefits (e.g., a lower cost of capital to firms, a higher return to saving, better diversification and consumption-smoothing in the face of external shocks, and stronger market discipline against errant domestic policies), it also makes them more susceptible to financial shocks originating elsewhere. Such contagion is apt to be stronger during crisis periods than at other times. Vulnerability to contagion is apt to be greatest, other things being equal, for smaller emerging market economies, for countries inhabiting the same region as the original crisis country, for countries that share similar characteristics with the crisis country, and for countries whose earlier and present track record on policy fundamentals is relatively weak.

CONCLUDING REMARKS

In developing an early warning system for financial crises in emerging economies, work could proceed profitably along two fronts.

First, a systematic effort should be made to determine which emerging market economies appear to be the most vulnerable to financial crises under a full set of indicators. Put in other words, one would attempt to see how much overlap there was among the "most vulnerable" list of countries thrown up by the individual indicators. Along similar lines, one could seek to develop a "composite" indicator that would weight the individual indicators by their relative reliability in forecasting crises. This would also help to compensate for the limited predictive power of individual indicators.[59] The objective would be to obtain a rough and ready "watch list" of countries for the medium term.

Second, there should be handsome returns to extending the econometric analyses of the past predictive performance of early warning indicators. This work is still in relatively early stages but has already generated some interesting results. Two of the most useful studies for the purpose of this paper are Frankel and Rose (1995) and Kaminsky and Reinhart (1996). These studies allow one to examine a much larger sample of currency and banking crises than could be accommodated by case studies, they provide some evidence on the relative ranking of the predictive performance of individual indicators, and they offer a clue about how accurate (inaccurate) even the best of the indicators would have been in predicting currency and banking crises over the past three decades.

Frankel and Rose (1995) use a panel of data for over 100 developing countries during the 1971-1992 period. They restrict their attention to currency crashes, defined as a large change in the nominal exchange rate (at least 25 percent) that is also a substantial increase in the rate of change of the nominal depreciation rate (exceeding the previous year's change by at least 25 percent).[60] This yields 117 different currency events. Their goal is to see which variables help predict these currency crashes. Graphical analysis, and univariate and multivariate regression techniques are employed.

Among Frankel and Rose's more interesting findings are the following: (i) an increase in foreign interest rates, a high external debt burden, a high degree of real exchange rate overvaluation, the onset of recession, and a high rate of domestic credit creation each increase vulnerability to a crash;[61] (ii) a larger stock of international reserves decreases vulnerability, while large current ac-

---

[59] Frankel and Rose (1995) conclude in their analysis of over 100 currency crashes in developing countries that "... there is not that much information in any single indicator variable considered alone." (p. 35).

[60] Because of this definition of a currency crash, Frankel and Rose (1995) are unable to include in their sample speculative attacks that were successfully warded off.

[61] Frankel and Rose (1995) measure overvaluation as the deviation of the real exchange rate from its period average. Supporting the arguments made in the second part of this paper, they also conclude that the combination of high indebtedness with an increase in foreign interest rates seems to be a recipe for a currency crash.

count and fiscal deficits show mixed results; (iii) the composition of capital inflows matters, with vulnerability being higher with higher shares of short-term, variable rate, portfolio capital, foreign-currency denominated, and commercial debt in the total;[62] (iv) the composition variable with the best predictive performance is the share of foreign direct investment (the higher the share, the lower the vulnerability to a crisis); and (v) controls on current account convertibility do not seem to reduce vulnerability.

Kaminsky and Reinhart (1996) examine both balance-of-payments and banking crises for a sample of 14 developing and 5 (small) industrial countries over a period that spans the 1970s through the early 1990s. Balance-of-payments crises are defined in terms of extreme values of an index of currency turbulence (which is, in turn, a weighted average of exchange rate changes and of changes in international reserves). Banking crises are defined as events marked either by bank runs or by closure, merging, takeover, or extension of large-scale government assistance to important financial institutions (with spillover effects to other financial firms).

In addition to summarizing the stylized facts surrounding crises, Kaminsky and Reinhart (1996) investigate the signaling ability of alternative indicators in terms, inter alia, of the noise-to-signal ratio (i.e., the ratio of inaccurate to accurate signals). Among their noteworthy findings are the following: (i) banking crises help to predict currency crises, whereas the converse is not true; (ii) capital-account variables (not surprisingly) do better in predicting balance-of-payments crises after financial liberalization than before it; (iii) on the whole, the best indicators for predicting balance-of-payments crises are appreciations of the real exchange rate (relative to trend), changes in export receipts, declines in the stock market, domestic recessions, and the ratio of a broad monetary aggregate (M2) to international reserves; (iv) as for banking crises, the best of the pack seems to be (again) appreciation of the real exchange rate, a sinking stock market, an increase in the money multiplier (as a proxy for financial liberal-

---

[62] Frankel and Rose's (1995) debt composition results suggest that emerging markets have dangerous debt characteristics when they hit 17 percent in commercial loans, 19 percent at variable rates; 75 percent in public-sector loans; 14 percent short-term debt; or 1 percent foreign direct investment flows.

ization), domestic recession, and an increase in the domestic real interest rate;[63] and (v) even the best early warning indicators send at least two to three wrong signals for every correct one, and for most indicators, the signal-to-noise ratio is much higher than that—reinforcing the high-risk nature of the exercise itself.

It is encouraging that these econometric studies generally support the outcomes expected from economic theory. These studies also confirm the relevance of the seven indicators outlined here, albeit with three nuances: (i) it is quite likely that recession is an underlying factor in several of the indicators and thus should be accorded substantial weight in signaling both currency and banking crises; (ii) stock market declines, even when unaccompanied by bank lending booms, seem to have significant predictive power for detecting banking crises in emerging markets; and (iii) export receipts may have additional signaling power for balance-of-payments crises beyond any contribution to current account imbalances.

It is not difficult to see at least five promising extensions of this econometric work on financial crises. First (as suggested earlier), in analyzing the role of current account imbalances as a presumptive indicator, account should be taken of the way foreign borrowing is used and financed. Adjusting current account positions for the investment/consumption mix and for the maturity of financing may well lead to better results than have been obtained so far for raw current account imbalances. Second, one should likewise include in the analysis the amounts and kinds of assistance available from other governments at times of crisis. Take the case of a currency crisis. Not only can strong-currency governments add to the defending country's international liquidity by providing (contingent) lines of credit in foreign exchange; they can also reduce the weak currency's need for large increases in its domestic interest rate by reducing their own interest rates. Countries that can count on substantial, quick outside assistance will, ceteris paribus, be less vulnerable to attack than those that cannot.

---

[63] In many cases of financial liberalization, banks' reserve requirements are reduced, thereby leading to a rise in the money multiplier.

Third, we need an operational measure of speculative attacks on currencies in emerging markets that will allow us to include in the sample speculative attacks against which governments made *successful* defenses: the lessons there may be as valuable as those associated with unsuccessful defenses. Fourth, on the banking crisis side, real estate prices should be brought into the picture (data permitting). They feature in too many banking crises to be excluded from the statistical tests. Finally, indicators of liquidity mismatches in government debt management need to be made more forward looking. If, for example, there is a widely known bunching of maturities six months hence that is likely to be large in relation to the stock of reserves at that point, this could well affect market pressures now (even though it wouldn't be reflected in today's debt or debt-service numbers).

All this is a tall order. But we are unlikely to move from 20/20 hindsight to having some foresight about financial crises in emerging markets by standing pat.

REFERENCES

Artus, Patrick et al. 1995. "The Emerging Economies: Vulnerability and Potential." Caisse des Depots et Consignations, *Economic Notes*. November.

Balino, Tomas, and V. Sundararajan, eds. 1991. *Banking Crises: Cases and Issues*. Washington, D.C.: IMF.

Calvo, Guillermo, and Morris Goldstein. 1996. "Crisis Prevention and Crisis Management After Mexico: What Role for the Official Sector?" In *Private Capital Flows to Emerging Markets After the Mexican Crisis*, edited by Guillermo Calvo, Morris Goldstein, and Edward Hochreiter. Washington, D.C.: Institute for International Economics. September, pp. 233-282.

Calvo, Guillermo, Leonardo Leidermann, and Carmen Reinhart. 1994. "The Capital Inflows Problem: Concepts and Issues. "*Contemporary Economic Policy*, vol. 12, July, pp. 54-66.

Calvo, Guillermo, Leonardo Leidermann, and Carmen Reinhart. 1993. "Capital Inflows and Real Exchange Rate Appreciation in Latin America: The Role of External Factors." IMF *Staff Papers*, vol. 40, no. 1, pp. 108-150.

Calvo, Guillermo, Ratna Sahay, and Carlos Vegh. 1996. "Capital Flows in Central and Eastern Europe." In *Private Capital Flows to Emerging Markets After the Mexican Crisis*, edited by G. Calvo, M. Goldstein, and E. Hochreiter. Washington, D.C.: Institute for International Economics. September, pp. 57-90.

Calvo, Sara, and Carmen Reinhart. 1996. "Capital Flows to Latin America: Is There Evidence of Contagion Effects?" In *Private Capital Flows to Emerging Markets After the Mexican Crisis*, edited by G. Calvo, M. Goldstein, and E. Hochreiter. Washington, D.C.: Institute for International Economics. pp. 151-171.

Caprio, Gerard, and Daniela Klingebiel. 1996. "Bank Insolvencies: Cross-Country Experience." Washington, D.C.: World Bank. (unpublished)

Caprio, Gerard, Izak Atiyas, and James Hanson. 1994. *Financial Reform: Theory and Experience*. Cambridge: Cambridge University Press.

Chuhan, Punam, Stijn Claessens, and Niandu Mamingi. 1993. "Equity and Bond Flows to Latin America and Asia: The Role of Global and Country Factors." World Bank Policy Research Paper No. 1160. Washington, D.C.: World Bank, July.

Claessens, Stijn, Michael Dooley, and Andrew Warner. 1993. "Portfolio Capital Flows: Hot or Cool?" In *Portfolio Investment in Developing Countries*, edited by S. Claessens and S. Cooptu. Washington, D.C.: World Bank.

Clark, Peter, Leonardo Bartolini, Tamim Bayoumi, and Steven Symansky. 1994. "Exchange Rates and Economic Fundamentals." IMF *Occasional Paper* No. 115. Washington, D.C.: IMF.

Cline, William. 1995. "Capital Markets After the Peso Crisis." Paper presented at the Annual World Bank Conference on "Development in Latin America and the Caribbean." Rio de Janeiro, June 12-13.

Dooley, Michael, Eduardo Fernandez-Arias, and Kenneth Kletzer. 1994. "Recent Private Capital Inflows to Developing Countries: Is the Debt Crisis History?" NBER Working Paper No. 4792. Cambridge: National Bureau of Economic Research, July.

Edwards, Sebastian. 1994. "Real and Monetary Determinants of Real Exchange Rate Behavior." In *Estimating Equilibrium Exchange Rates*, edited by John Williamson. Washington, D.C.: Institute for International Economics. pp. 61-92.

Eichengreen, Barry. 1995. *International Monetary Arrangements for the 21st Century*. Washington, D.C.: Brookings Institution.

Eisenbeis, Robert. 1995. "Systemic Risk: Bank Deposits and Credit." In *Research in Financial Services*, edited by G. Kaufman. Greenwich: JAI Press. (forthcoming)

Elbadawi, Ibraham. 1994. "Estimating Long-Run Equilibrium Exchange Rates" In *Estimating Equilibrium Exchange Rates*, edited by

John Williamson. Washington, D.C.: Institute for International Economics. pp. 93-132.

Fernandez-Arias, Eduardo. 1994. "The New Wave of Private Capital Inflows: Push or Pull?" World Bank Policy Research Paper No. 1312. Washington, D.C.: World Bank.

Fernandez-Arias, Eduardo, and Peter Montiel. 1995. "The Surge in Private Capital Inflows to Developing Countries." World Bank Policy Research Paper No. 1473. Washington, D.C.: World Bank.

Fischer, Stanley. 1994. "Comment on Dornbusch." *Brookings Papers on Economic Activity,* 1994:1.

Frankel, Jeffrey. 1995. "Have Latin American and Asian Countries So Liberalized Capital Inflows That Sterilization Is Now Impossible?" Paper presented at the World Bank-American Finance Association Special Session at the annual AEA/AFA meetings, Washington, D.C., December.

Frankel, Jeffrey, and Andrew Rose. 1995. "Exchange Rate Crashes in Emerging Markets: An Empirical Treatment." Berkeley: Economics Department, University of California at Berkeley. (unpublished)

Frenkel, Jacob, Morris Goldstein, and Paul Masson. 1991. "Characteristics of a Successful Exchange Rate System." IMF *Occasional Paper* No. 82. Washington, D.C.: IMF.

Garber, Peter, and Lars Svensson. 1995. "The Operation and Collapse of Fixed Exchange Rate Regimes." In *Handbook of International Economics,* edited by G. Grossman and K. Rogoff. vol. III, Amsterdam: North-Holland.

Gavin, Michael, and Ricardo Hausman. 1995. "The Macroeconomic Roots of Banking Crises." Paper presented at IADB conference on "Banking Crises in Latin America." Washington, D.C., October.

Goldstein, Morris. 1997. *The Case for an International Banking Standard,* Policy Analyses in International Economics No. 47. Washington, D.C.: Institute for International Economics.

Goldstein, Morris. 1995a. "International Financial Markets and Economics. (unpublished)

Goldstein, Morris. 1995b. "Coping with Too Much of a Good Thing: Policy Responses for Large Capital Inflows in Developing Countries." World Bank Policy Research Working Paper No. 1507. Washington, D.C.: World Bank.

Goldstein, Morris, et al. 1993a. *International Capital Markets Report: Exchange Rate Management and International Capital Flows.* IMF World Economic and Financial Surveys. Washington, D.C.: IMF.

Goldstein, Morris, et al. 1993b. *International Capital Markets Report: Systemic Issues in International Finance,* IMF World Economic and Financial Surveys. Washington, D.C.: IMF.

Goldstein, Morris, and Michael Mussa. 1994. "The Integration of World Capital Markets." In Federal Reserve Bank of Kansas City, *Changing Capital Markets*. Kansas City: Federal Reserve Bank of Kansas City, pp. 245-314.

Goldstein, Morris, and Philip Turner. 1996. "Banking Crises in Emerging Economies: Origins and Policy Options." *BIS Economic Papers*. No. 46. Basle: Bank for International Settlements, October.

Honohan, Patrick. 1996."Financial Systems Failures in Developing Countries: Diagnosis and Prediction." Washington, D.C.: International Monetary Fund, June. (unpublished)

International Monetary Fund. 1995. *International Capital Markets Report: Developments, Prospects, and Policy Issues*. Washington, D.C.: IMF, August.

Kaminsky, Graciela, and Carmen Reinhart. 1996. "The Twin Crises: The Causes of Banking and Balance of Payments Problems." International Finance Discussion Paper No. 544. Washington, D.C.: Board of Governors of the Federal Reserve System, March.

Kindleberger, Charles. 1978. *Manics, Panics, and Crashes*. New York: Basic Books.

Krugman, Paul. 1991. "Financial Crises in the International Economy." In *The Risk of Economic Crisis*, edited by M. Feldstein. Chicago: University of Chicago Press, pp. 85-108.

Krugman, Paul. 1985. "Is the Strong Dollar Sustainable?" In Federal Reserve Bank of Kansas City, *The U.S. Dollar: Recent Developments, Outlook, and Policy Options*. Kansas City: Federal Reserve Bank of Kansas City, pp. 103-132.

Krugman, Paul. 1979. "A Model of Balance-of-Payments Crises." *Journal of Money, Credit, and Banking*, vol. 11, pp. 311-325.

Leiderman, Leonardo, and Alfredo Thorne. 1996. "The 1994 Mexican Crisis and its Aftermath: What Are the Main Lessons?" In *Private Capital Flows to Emerging Markets After the Mexican Crisis*, edited by G. Calvo, M. Goldstein, and E. Hochreiter. Washington, D.C.: Institute for International Economics, September, pp. 1-43.

Ludwig, Eugene. 1994. "Supervising an Evolving Industry." Federal Reserve Bank of Chicago, *Bank Structure and Competition*.

Marris, Stephen. 1985. *Deficits and the Dollar*. Policy Analysis in International Economics No. 14. Washington, D.C.: Institute for International Economics, September.

Mishkin, Frederick. 1994. "Preventing Financial Crises: An International Perspective." NBER Working Paper No. 4636. Cambridge: National Bureau of Economic Research, February.

Obstfeld, Maurice, and Ken Rogoff. 1995. "The Mirage of Fixed Exchange

Rates." *Journal of Economic Perspectives*, vol. 9, no. 4, pp. 73-96.

Portes, Richard. 1991. "Comment on Federov." In *Currency Convertibility in Eastern Europe*, edited by John Williamson. Washington, D.C.: Institute for International Economics, pp. 328-331.

Rojas-Suarez, Liliana, and Steven Weisbrod. 1995. "Managing Banking Crises in Latin America: The Do's and Don'ts of Successful Bank Restructuring Programs." Paper presented at IADB conference on "Banking Crises in Latin America." Washington, D.C., October.

Rose, Andrew, and Lars Svensson. 1994. "European Exchange Rate Credibility Before the Fall." *European Economic Review*, vol. 38, June, pp. 1185-1216.

Sachs, Jeffrey, Aaron Tornell, and Andres Velasco. 1995. "The Collapse of the Mexican Peso: What Have We Learned?" Cambridge: Economics Department, Harvard University, May.

Schwartz, Anna. 1986. "Real and Pseudo Financial Crises." In *Financial Crises and the World Banking System*, edited by F. Capie and G. Wood. London: Macmillan. pp. 11-31.

Svensson, Lars. 1991. "The Simplest Test of Target Zone Credibility." IMF *Staff Papers*, vol. 38, September, pp. 655-665.

U.S. Treasury. 1995. *Semi-Annual Report to Congress by the Secretary of the Treasury on behalf of the President: Pursuant to the Mexican Debt Disclosure Act of 1995.* Washington, D.C.: U.S. Treasury, December.

Williamson, John. 1996. "Comment on Borrowing in International Capital Markets." In *Private Capital Flows to Emerging Markets After the Mexican Crisis*, edited by G. Calvo, M. Goldstein, and E. Hochreiter. Washington, D.C.: Institute for International Economics, pp. 112-114.

Williamson, John. 1994. *Estimating Equilibrium Exchange Rates.* Washington, D.C.: Institute for International Economics.

CHAPTER SEVEN

SUMMARY OF DISCUSSION

PRIYA BASU AND MARIAN BOND

COMMENTS

RONALD I. McKINNON
William Eberly Professor of International Economics,
Stanford University

In his comments, Ronald McKinnon focused on three broad themes that, he noted, had been and continue to be an important part of financial sector development: first, banking sector and related issues (the PRC and Indonesia) and their relationship to state enterprise losses and monetary control in the PRC; second, issues related to greater disclosure by banks as a movement toward more self-regulation (New Zealand); and third, macro issues related to overborrowing in Asia and to the issue of sequencing of financial sector reforms (PRC, Indonesia, and New Zealand).

First, he noted that, when the PRC embarked on financial sector reforms in 1978, there was a need for a major deconsolidation of the monobank. The government spun off the central bank, various commercial banks, and savings banks from the monobank, and then started to commercialize some of the rural cooperatives and other credit operations. That was accompanied by price stability in the PRC in the 1980s, and by remarkable financial deepening.

The increase in the real demand for financial assets had been tremendous, rising from about RMB40 per person to an average of RMB3,000 per person by 1995. The M2/GNP ratio had risen to over 100 percent in 1996, having started in the order of 20 percent in 1978, and that excluded all new securities that had been issued. This remarkable financialization of the PRC's economy, it was noted, was on a level with what had occurred in Taipei,China in the 1960s and 1970s, and in Japan in the 1950s and 1960s during their period of very high financial growth in those countries.

The difference between the PRC today and Taipei,China and Japan earlier, he pointed out, was in the nature of the fiscal process. McKinnon noted that the PRC had not exactly followed the order of economic liberalization suggested in his work,[1] and because of the nature of its transition from a centrally planned economy to a market economy, there had been a natural tendency for the revenue position of the government to erode somewhat rapidly. In the case of the PRC, it was the revenue position of the central government that was eroded rather than that of the provinces or local governments. This situation had created very large fiscal deficits throughout the 1980s, both in terms of what was needed to finance government consumption and in terms of the policy loans that were required to prop up loss-making state-owned enterprises (SOEs) or to finance infrastructure needs that did not meet market criteria.

Therefore, a considerable share of the huge financialization of the economy was lent back to the government and became a fiscal support mechanism as well as a mechanism for financing much decentralized investment. The problem with that kind of fiscal support in McKinnon's view was that it limited the pace at which the PRC's financial system could be liberalized. For example, the system had operated for a long time with very high implicit reserve requirements on the agricultural credit cooperatives and around two thirds of the bank deposits of farmers were actually passed back to the government in one way or another (more recently, the proportion has fallen to around one

---

[1] The order of economic liberalization as laid out in the works of McKinnon and Dornbusch is discussed in Chapter 1.

third). Those very high reserve requirements on the banking system (some of them implicit, some more formal) limited the pace at which the banking system could be commercialized. If commercialization had proceeded at a faster pace, the government's fiscal deficit would have been uncovered and the result could have been an inflationary explosion. He went on to say that the authorities in the PRC were well aware of this fiscal restraint and that they had introduced quite remarkable tax reforms to deal with it. Nonetheless, fiscal considerations continued to set limits on the speed of financial liberalization at the macro level because reforming too fast would have led to an inflation problem.

When considering the deconsolidation of the monobank into various decentralized entities at the micro level, McKinnon drew attention to the differences between entities with regard to the soft budget constraint syndrome in the PRC. The point was illustrated by looking at township village enterprises (TVEs) and the SOEs. TVEs, on the one hand, are owned by townships and villages, and as such, they do not have special access to the banks, do not appoint bank managers, and do not have much authority over the banks. Thus, although TVEs borrow from the banks, they are not guaranteed soft policy loans and it is possible for them to go bankrupt. SOEs, on the other hand, are government-owned industrial corporations at the county, province, and central levels of government. Historically, they have had very soft budget constraints because at that level, the officials in the government of counties and provinces appoint the staff of the major banks and can order them to make loans to loss-making enterprises.

McKinnon stressed that one of the main objectives of the deconsolidation or commercialization of the banking system should be to harden the budget constraint on the SOEs. That could be done by taking away the authority of middle-level governments over the banks and insulating the governments as much as possible from decision making. He said he was unclear how successful this had been in the PRC. Three banks had been set up to take over the soft policy loans with a view to leaving the regular industrial banks, also known as specialized banks, to be the hard-loan window. The success of this policy would be extremely important for the PRC.

On the issue of monetary control in the PRC, McKinnon noted that because of the size of the PRC, the exchange rate could not be used as an intermediate target as in New Zealand. At the same time, he noted that with the major transformation of the financial system in the PRC, all the monetary aggregates had grown extremely fast so they could not be used as intermediate targets either. McKinnon said that although it would be good to move as fast as possible toward indirect methods of monetary control, generally speaking, direct credit restrictions would remain very important for monetary control and macro stability in the PRC for many years to come, particularly where middle-level government was involved.

Turning to Indonesia, McKinnon drew attention to the rapid rate of growth in the banking sector in Indonesia following the complete liberalization of entry into banking under the *PAKTO* reforms. The number of banks had increased from 124 in 1978 to 240 in 1995, and the number of bank branches had increased from 1,900 in 1978 to 6,000. While he did not doubt the benefits of those developments, he did note, however, that there were considerable opportunity costs associated with such a major liberalization of the banking system, in terms of a *"decline in the franchise value of the existing banks."* In other words, he argued that as long as entry into banking and the number of licenses for branches were limited, there was a high franchise value, where the effective ownership or goodwill in the bank was greater than the formal capital that appeared on the books. That made banks conservative because if they went bankrupt, they would lose a stream of monopoly rents into the future. Once the system was liberalized completely, as was being done in Indonesia, the future stream of monopoly rents and the franchise value would be reduced, and that would render banks more prone to risky behavior unless capital requirements and prudential regulations were in place. That seemed to be happening in Indonesia where, in 1991, the system was restructured to make the capital requirements tougher than they would otherwise have been.

Second, on the remarkable deregulation of the banks in New Zealand—an exercise in corporate governance—McKinnon thought that, in general, policy makers in the United States and the United Kingdom should make directors more responsible and accountable, and that this should not be confined to just the banking system, as with the Brash reforms. McKinnon liked the idea of having quarterly reports and having full information about the capital positions of the bank. He would add to matters to be disclosed what he called the *"duration gap"*—the gap in the term to maturity between assets and liabilities. He would also add disclosure on the openness of foreign exchange positions, although he noted that those positions could change very rapidly. All disclosures should become public information, and the information would be extremely useful in terms of making the banking system more accountable.

In McKinnon's view, New Zealand has an implicit deposit insurance in the banking system in that the New Zealand government has a basic commitment to support the payments mechanism. The system is thus not the same as an industrial corporation with directors accountable for the risk. While he conceded that the new system could help make full information available to the public and thus enable the public to make its own decisions regarding the choices of banks, there was still room for prudential regulation.

Third, regarding the excess accumulation of foreign exchange reserves in the PRC, McKinnon noted that the holdings amounted to US$80 billion,[2] with the bulk of the reserves held in United States Treasury bonds. He questioned whether that reflected overborrowing. Referring to his recent paper entitled "Credible Liberalizations and International Capital Flows—the Overborrowing Syndrome," McKinnon recounted the experiences of Mexico and Chile. The huge inflow of capital into Mexico in the early 1990s and into Chile in the late 1970s, he noted, had led to an overvalued currency, excess lending for consumption, and, finally, a crash. In asking whether Asian economies were similarly vulnerable to the overborrowing syndrome in the sense defined above, he argued that most Asian economies were better insulated against it, partly because the flow of finance through the banking systems in countries such as Malaysia, Thailand, and the PRC (countries that might be vulnerable) was much less consumption-oriented than it had been in Latin Amercia during the

---

[2] Currently the PRC's holding of foreign exchange reserves is estimated at over US$100 billion.

boom. He cautioned that although liberalizing the banking system was very important, the banking system should not be liberalized to the point that it becomes very easy to get consumer credit. Large capital inflows used for consumption purposes would tend to bring about results such as the Mexican debacle. Private saving in Mexico, unlike in the Asian countries referred to, fell to a half from 1988 to 1994, fueled by an enormous inflow of capital. McKinnon stated that, as he understood it, the buildup of real assets in the PRC was not a problem (he did not think that the exchange rate was overvalued); nevertheless, it was something to watch out for. He reflected that it might be more of a problem for Thailand or Malaysia as Paul Dickie had pointed out earlier.

Moving on to New Zealand, McKinnon noted that he was very pleased to see that Donald Brash was still Governor of the Reserve Bank of New Zealand (RBNZ), despite the fact that the rate of inflation in New Zealand was 2.1 percent, a little above the target. He noted that Brash was responsible for much of the extraordinary reform that had occurred and had made New Zealand the most market oriented of the OECD economies. However, he observed that in the remarkable transformation that had taken place over the past 20 years, New Zealand had not succeeded in getting the order of liberalization quite right. When New Zealand started liberalizing in 1984, it liberalized the capital account and exchange controls first, along with some attempts to rationalize foreign trade. However, a large fiscal haemorrhage remained and the labor market was still fairly well regulated with considerable state intervention. One of the consequences of not getting the order of liberalization right was that there was a big capital inflow, partly to finance the fiscal deficit, and the currency was overvalued for the initial years of liberalization. This resulted in extremely slow growth and doubts that the liberalization would succeed politically. But fortunately, as events unfolded, political considerations supported the reform process. McKinnon noted that the liberalization had succeeded and that the New Zealand economy was growing very rapidly.

Another interesting aspect of New Zealand's experience, McKinnon noted, was the use of the exchange rate. Brash had mentioned in his presentation that New Zealand was the only country that had not, for 11 years, intervened in the foreign exchange market to influence the exchange rate. McKinnon agreed that they had not intervened directly, but noted that they had geared their monetary policy very much toward targeting the exchange rate as a kind of an intermediate variable. Although the price level target was very definite, he thought that the exchange rate had been used as a sort of intermediate variable. The way it worked was that interest rates were adjusted. That, in turn, influenced the exchange rate, which influenced prices. He noted that the exchange rate had been very much a part of the monetary process, and in a small open economy like New Zealand, it had been very successful as a control device.

One of the big successes that he thought had been a little underrated in New Zealand was that the reforms had put terrific restraints on the fiscal authorities, because the authorities knew that if there was any loss of fiscal control, RBNZ would be forced to tighten money and the currency would rise in the foreign exchanges, making farmers and exporters very unhappy. McKinnon pointed out that there had been strong popular pressure on countries to run fiscal surpluses because of the hard money nature of the monetary regime. He was not sure whether the New Zealand system had been designed with that intent, but it seemed to be an important outcome of New Zealand's experience.

Turning to Indonesia, McKinnon drew attention to the recovery from the great neo-hyperinflations and to the extremely repressive policies of the 1960s. He supported the point that Indonesia did not get the order of liberalization exactly right, with the opening up of the capital account coming first. But he described that as "an artifact of the oil enclave." Because the currency was unnaturally strong and Indonesia was so dependent on oil exports in the 1970s, there had been a desire by the government to weaken the currency in the foreign exchanges by removing restrictions on capital outflows. But he noted that when a country removes restrictions, the currency becomes more attractive, and policy makers may not ultimately get the desired result. What interested McKinnon was that a fall in the price of oil, both in 1982 and 1986, had been required to break the oil enclave problem. Those events had led to much more serious and deeper internal reforms in the Indonesian economy, and although it seemed like a disaster at the time, he noted that it had turned out to be a very good thing for Indonesia.

COMMENTS

MORRIS GOLDSTEIN
*Dennis Weatherstone Senior Fellow, Institute of
International Economics, Washington, D.C.*

In his remarks, Morris Goldstein put the issues already discussed into a broader perspective by concentrating on five themes: first, the sequencing of financial reforms; second, the strengthening of banking supervision; third, the development of government bond markets; fourth, the role of, and limits to, transparency and disclosure; and fifth, early warning signals in financial crisis.

In reflecting on the issues related to sequencing of financial reforms, Goldstein noted that there existed a lively debate over whether the banking sector or the nonbanking financial sector ought to be given priority. Whatever the outcome of that debate, Goldstein mentioned at least four propositions that he believed commanded quite wide consensus.

First, in the foreseeable future, banks were going to play perhaps a declining but nevertheless important role as financial intermediaries. He noted that Paul Dickie had pointed out that in most Asian developing countries, bank assets typically accounted for 60 to 75 percent of total financial assets.

Second, where there were surges of private capital flows into Asian developing countries, the bulk of these were intermediated by the banking system.

Third, even when the aim was to develop securities markets rapidly, this would be difficult to do without the assistance of a strong banking system. Securities markets needed lines of credit from banks to deal with temporary liquidity shortages. In addition, securities exchanges and clearinghouses relied on banks to finance margin calls, and banks, along with the central bank, were crucial in operating the payments system.

Fourth, Goldstein noted that recent experience was full of examples where financial liberalization without prior strengthening of banking supervision soon produced a banking crisis and large public sector bailout costs. He noted that generally, when banking crises had occurred, the costs were large. The

Savings and Loan debacle in the United States cost US$150 billion to US$200 billion, the ongoing bad loan problem in Japan had cost approximately US$400 billion to US$600 billion, the banking crisis in Scandinavia cost somewhere between 3 and 7 percent of GDP before resolution. He also noted that there had been some banking crises in developing countries where the cost had been as high as 10 percent of GDP, or even more.

Given the large costs of banking crises, Goldstein stressed the importance of strengthening banking supervision. In his view, five main areas merited explicit mention. First, there should be strict disclosure on, and limits for, connected lending, i.e., lending by the bank to bank owners and directors and their related businesses. Without such limits, banks were courting excessive concentration of credit risk and, in addition, connected lending carried the danger that loans to insiders might not be extended on arm's-length terms.

Second, there should be greater transparency in, and possible direct limits on, government-directed lending via the commercial banks, compulsory holding by commercial banks of short-term government securities at less than market rates, and payment below market interest rates on commercial banks' reserve assets. Goldstein pointed out that those techniques represented taxes on the banking system and were quasi-fiscal activities of the government. He mentioned that Li Rougu in his paper had documented that the PRC had moved in the direction of reducing such practices over time by, for example, having the state-owned specialized banks embark on the road to commercialization while leaving the newly created policy-oriented banks to take over subsidized lending requested by the government.

Third, systems of credit classification and provisioning should not only classify loans based on their payments performance but also on the repayment capacity and riskiness of the borrower. Goldstein pointed out that by using only payments performance for credit classification, bank supervisors could allow the banks to keep bad loans evergreen by rolling them over. If a bank had a bad loan and the borrower could not pay, the bank would make another loan, restructure the loan at low interest rates, and thereby the borrower's loan remained current and did not have to be listed as nonperforming. Under this arrangement the bank would still have its capital and everything would look good. In reality,

Goldstein pointed out that such a loan was bad and the true capital would be significantly lower than stated. He noted the need for bank supervisors to go beyond payments performance in assessing the creditworthiness of banks.

Fourth, banks had to hold adequate capital not only to meet credit risk but also to deal with market risk that might be associated with unexpected changes in exchange rates, interest rates, inflation rates, real estate prices, and the terms of trade.

Fifth, and what Goldstein considered to be the most important point for many developing countries, was the need to give consideration to prompt corrective action guidelines to spell out what remedial measures bank supervisors must impose on banks if their capital dropped below prespecified zones. The point of giving the supervisor less discretion and more rule-based guidance was to limit incentives to grant forbearance to troubled banks. The regulator should be prevented from gambling for resurrection. Goldstein explained that this term was usually applied to troubled banks, but the term also applied to regulators. He elaborated by saying that banking supervisors had to be given the authority to tell an influential banker that under the banking law there was no choice but to restrict the bank's activities because its capital had dropped into a zone where such actions were mandatory. The United States moved to this type of rule-based model of banking supervision after the Savings and Loan debacle, and it was one of the key provisions of the 1991 FDICIA (Federal Deposit Insurance Corporation Improvement Act). Goldstein observed that during the previous decade, more and more countries had come to appreciate the advantages of a politically independent central bank and he felt that the time had come to give similar attention to politically independent banking supervision.

Goldstein next turned to the issue of government bond markets and noted that Paul Dickie had emphasized the importance of developing markets for long-term debt in Asia. He looked at the example of an Asian country that wanted to sell a considerable amount of government debt at low cost to international institutional investors and asked what the country would need to do beyond just having good macroeconomic fundamentals. He felt the short answer to be that the country should undertake measures that enhanced the liquidity transfer and predictability of that bond market, and mentioned three related reform measures.

First, the country should consider having primary dealers, in other words, designated financial institutions with the obligation to place reasonable bids in government bond auctions and to create a continuous secondary market in a range of issues. Primary dealers were there to underpin liquidity. However, he noted that it would be very unlikely that a primary dealer system would add much to the market for US government securities because, even if there were no primary dealer system, people would still buy US Treasuries. But his point was that in thinner, much less liquid government bond markets, the potential benefits of a primary dealer system would be more significant.

Second, a country should consider moving toward larger issue sizes in a few benchmark securities. Again, the primary motivation would be liquidity, and the larger the issue, the greater its liquidity. Other fixed income securities, especially corporate bonds, could be priced with reference to those benchmarks. Again, issue size would likely be more important in thinner markets where there might not be enough investor demand to spread across a wide spectrum of issues.

Third, a country should consider removing the tax bias against bonds. In this context, Goldstein noted that taxes such as withholding taxes, turnover taxes, and stamp duties that are often imposed on bonds (but not on equities or bank deposits), can impede trade and result in segmented markets and reduced liquidity. Not surprisingly, such a tax bias against bonds is much disliked by institutional investors. He noted that policy makers who presided over the fiscal deficit sometimes argued that the revenue loss from eliminating these taxes could not be tolerated. However, he felt this argument was less than convincing because the extra borrowing costs stemming from the tax were often more than the revenue raised. In this connection, Goldstein said that he understood that when New Zealand removed its withholding tax, the reduction in interest rates on government borrowing was significant enough to make up for the year's lost tax revenue within the first few weeks of trading.

Goldstein next moved to the questions of transparency and disclosure which, he noted, had been "hot issues" over the past year. In this context, he drew attention to the recently launched

IMF Special Data Dissemination Standards. He also noted that pressures for greater disclosure of the bad loans of individual Japanese financial institutions had been prompted by the emergence of the Japan premium in the interbank market. He cited a host of initiatives that had been taken to increase disclosure for derivatives-related exposure. He also noted New Zealand's market-oriented approach to bank supervision. He felt that the driving force behind the move to greater transparency and disclosure was the recognition that private market discipline was increasingly important in restraining errant borrowers, and that private market discipline would not work unless creditors had access to comprehensive and timely information on the creditworthiness of borrowers.

While Goldstein pushed for transparency of disclosure during the financial sector transition process, he expressed the view that it would be going too far to suggest that full disclosure and full information were sufficient conditions for preventing financial crises. He recalled the background to the European Exchange Rate Mechanism (ERM) crisis, where, with the nominal anchor role of the exchange rate gaining increasing support within the ERM, and with prospects for the European Monetary Union (EMU) looking better and better, assets denominated in high interest rate ERM currencies, such as the lira and the peseta, looked like they were offering a supernormal rate of return. Investors thought that there was no risk of depreciation of those currencies and that they were getting a large premium over the return on, for example, deutsche mark assets. The cumulative position-taking embodied in these so-called convergence plays over the 1987 to 1992 period might have amounted to as much as US$300 billion. The trouble, of course, was that currency risk really had not gone away, and with the unexpected outcome of the Danish referendum, markets rethought their assumptions about currency risk and the inevitability of EMU, and the rush to the exits was soon in full swing.

Goldstein recounted similar events related to the bond market turbulence in industrial countries in early 1994, and the Mexican crisis. There too the crises were preceded by earlier successes and by large-scale position-taking based on the assumed scenario for interest rates and exchange rates, only to be upset by a massive shift in expectations. To sum up on this point, he pointed

out that disclosure and transparency did not eliminate the re-
peated tendency for market participants to take large, often highly
leveraged bets on the future costs of interest rates and exchange
rates, and to sometimes get it wrong. He noted that that was not
primarily a matter of information, but rather an attempt to make
a quick profit.

Finally, Goldstein addressed the question of which type of
early warning system would be useful in recognizing a financial
crisis in the making, whether it be a currency crisis, a banking
crisis, or a debt crisis. He suggested that the first response of an
economist to that question would probably be to look at interest
rate spreads. If a borrower were getting into trouble, the interest
rate spread on his obligations might be expected to continue to
widen out until finally the borrower would be denied access to
the market altogether. He noted, however, that an examination
of the behavior of interest rate spreads before several crises, including the Mexican crisis, the ERM crisis and some others,
showed that they did not provide a good early warning. He asked
what would give an early warning of financial crises if interest
rate spreads did not always do so. And in addressing that question, Goldstein listed seven early warning signals that he had
recently come up with, based on a review of the theoretical and
empirical literature on currency and banking crises in emerging
market countries. (These have been discussed in greater detail
in Chapter Six.)

First, an upward turn in international interest rates in the
main creditor or international markets, i.e., US interest rates,
LIBOR, SIBOR, etc. When those rates went up, assets in emerging markets became less attractive and the creditworthiness of
emerging market borrowers fell.

Second, a growing mismatch between a government's short-
term liquid liabilities and its international reserves, or between
the short-term liquid liabilities of the banking system and the
stock of international reserves.

The third early warning signal was a large current account
deficit used mainly for consumption, and financed in good measure by short-term borrowing.

Fourth, a highly overvalued real exchange rate, exacerbated
by the politicalization of exchange rate policy, often under a fixed
exchange rate regime.

Fifth, constraints related to financial fragility that limited the willingness to increase domestic interest rates, when there was a sharp falloff in private capital flows. A classic case was trouble in the banking system. Sweden had tried to raise overnight interest rates to 500 percent for a short period, but with a troubled banking system interest rates could not be increased for very long if the country had a large fiscal deficit with a large amount of floating rate debt. A country that had had seven or eight quarters of recession, as the UK had before the ERM crisis, would find it hard to push interest rates up for long.

The sixth early warning signal listed was an unsustainable boom in bank lending coupled with the collapse of real estate equity prices.

The seventh early warning signal according to Goldstein was high vulnerability to contagion of financial crises originating elsewhere.

COMMENTS

E.V.K. FITZGERALD
Director, Finance and Trade Policy Research Center,
International Development Center, Queen Elizabeth House,
Oxford University

E.V.K. FitzGerald focused on the macroeconomic side of financial liberalization and its international dimensions. He noted that three themes of post-financial liberalization had emerged from the proceedings. The first of these was the prudential regulation of banks and, by implication, nonbank financial intermediaries. Although the focus so far had been very much on the banks, he felt that there could be more problems in store in nonbank financial institutions that had not been exposed so far, as well as, by implication, in the functions of central banks as lender of last resort to keep the payments system going.

A second theme that had emerged was the changing relationship between fiscal and monetary policy, especially in terms of stocks and flows. These changing relationships had taken place as market segmentation had broken down and governments no longer had privileged access to either domestic savings or foreign exchange.

The third theme surrounded the question of how to manage short-term external capital flows. FitzGerald stated that most of the speakers seemed to be quite optimistic about moving away from a system of control in Asia, while he noted that in Latin Amercia there was a movement toward the reimposition of some forms of control in the form of reserve requirements and taxation. He went on to point out that one of the main pieces of evidence given in Latin America for reimposing controls was the enormous success in Asia of these controls. He felt it ironic that controls were being dismantled in Asia at the same time that they were being reimposed in Latin America.

He noted that the country papers presented at the seminar had provided examples of different responses to the three themes outlined as represented by very different stages of development, ranging from the PRC which was moving toward a full market economy but with a long way to go, to New Zealand with its full integration into the world economy. FitzGerald remarked that New Zealand's success story was, in large measure, due to the country's ability to use the international economy effectively as a regulatory mechanism for its own economy. He noted that, in contrast, the PRC was still to a great extent isolated from the world economy and therefore had to design its own system. In particular, the desire of the PRC to avoid stop-go cycles and the overheating of the economy, and to resolve its long-term SOE debt problem appeared to be a prelude to using international finance as an effective regulator of the domestic economy.

In this context, FitzGerald found it interesting that Indonesia wanted to retain a regulated system and also place reliance on moral suasion. He felt that carrying this out would require fairly concentrated and powerful domestic banks over which the authorities could impose some leverage. He added that full integration into the international financial system would make it more difficult for the authorities to operate a system of moral suasion of this sort.

FitzGerald recalled Ronald McKinnon's comments, noting that four danger points were brought up that reflected the early warning signals that Goldstein had indicated. He added that these four danger points focused on some of the international problems being faced by countries in Asia as they reform their financial systems, and that these had not been covered in previous discussions.

The first danger point was that the stability of Asian financial systems relied to a great extent on extremely high savings rates, particularly household or personal savings rates. FitzGerald felt that although the demand for assets by the private sector and households was very high in Asia, the demand for liabilities was also potentially very high. He noted that as a country liberalizes its financial system, the whole of the economy enters the world market and at the same time the demand for household credit tends to rise rapidly. He pointed out that much of the decline in domestic savings rates, or variations of domestic savings rates, both in Europe and Latin America, were due to fluctuations in household liabilities, while the demand for assets remained very stable. Given this evidence, he cautioned that Asia should not take for granted the currently very high household savings rates since these might not be a source of long-term investment funding. He felt that specific measures would probably have to be taken in the long run to protect that source of funds, because as soon as household savings rates fall and countries begin to rely on foreign capital for consumption finance, they could face the sort of problems that Mexico faced.

The second danger point that FitzGerald mentioned was that an over-appreciation of the exchange rate could lead to speculative capital inflows. If the exchange rate were fixed, or appeared to be steadily rising, then foreign funds would pour in to take advantage of the appreciation. He cautioned the audience that they may need to rethink the effect that this would have on the export sector. In the short run, real exchange rate appreciation could have a very positive effect by forcing industries to shake off excess labor or to make more effort to compete internationally by quality, instead of by price; however, it might be very difficult to sustain that approach for very long. One of the major differences between the experiences of Latin America and Asia, he noted, was the ability of Asia to keep real exchange rates stable and competitive, whereas Latin America had suffered from bouts of exchange rate appreciation. He felt that it would be very un-fortunate if monetary policy were designed in such a way as to allow for real exchange rate appreciation.

The third danger point was that it was generally thought that the long-run development function of a banking system and of nonbank financial intermediaries was to provide long-term capital support for investment in modern high-tech export manufacturing, and to fund the huge infrastructure requirements of the region. However, in FitzGerald's view, the sort of financial reforms the seminar had been discussing would not necessarily achieve that end. While they might lead to greater financial efficiency in terms of reducing margins, and to a greater entry of foreign investment, it was not clear whether they would support long-term corporate financial requirements. He stated that increasingly, evidence from other parts of the world showed that forced competition between banks and nonbank intermediaries led the banks to withdraw from long-term corporate finance in order to compete in the more highly liquid and profitable operations of lending to hedge funds, or lending for consumer finance.

FitzGerald commented that corporations had had difficulties in obtaining long-term finance at acceptable interest rates in a number of hedging markets, and that they had been driven to borrow abroad. The other side of the Mexican crisis, apart from consumer borrowing from overseas, was that Mexican companies had become very heavily indebted in the United States because of the comparatively lower interest rates. He noted that the consequence of that activity was that when a country devalued, companies off-loaded their bad debts on to the banks and that compounded the banking crisis. The Republic of Korea, for example, had successfully operated direct constraints (and continued to do so) not only on its banking system, but also on corporate borrowing overseas to stop that from happening. He was unsure whether that was the best solution to the problem, but he noted that countries should be concerned about not only tracking the financial performance of banks but also tracking the financial situation of large corporations. If he were to add an eighth indicator to Morris Goldstein's early warning indicators, he would include the exchange exposure and liquidity positions of large domestic corporations (the top 100 or so). It was very difficult to know whether a crisis was looming unless the foreign exchange and liquidity positions of both banks and large corporations were known.

It was well known that neither in the OECD countries nor in the Asian region were equity markets the fundamental source of long-term finance for corporations. FitzGerald believed that reinvestment of their own funds and, loans from banks would remain the fundamental sources of long-term finance for corporations in the foreseeable future, and, consequently, attention should be focused on both of those sources.

The fourth danger point that FitzGerald brought up was the issue of international cooperation in monetary and regulatory matters. He noted that, in a global economy where domestic funds could move out of a country and foreign funds could move in and out with ease, any regulatory regime or stabilization system must be an international one. He stressed that, in such environment, no individual country could successfully perform the regulatory task in isolation. He also noted that the region was moving toward monetary coordination, particularly in reserve management. An important item on the agenda should thus be to introduce some form of regional or international cooperation. He pointed out that supporting the ERM in its difficult moments had been immensely expensive for the Bundesbank. Putting together a bailout operation for Mexico had been difficult and expensive, and the Europeans had felt it should be a regional matter involving only the United States, whereas the United States had felt it was an international matter for all to cooperate on. He speculated on whether any future Asian financial crisis should be handled by regional organizations—in which case which organization would it be, who would fund it, and who would monitor the country; or whether it should be seen as the responsibility of a multilateral organization such as the IMF or the BIS.

RESPONSES FROM THE PANELISTS

Donald Brash agreed that McKinnon was absolutely right in stating that the sequencing of New Zealand's reforms had been wrong. He explained that it was widely recognized in New Zealand that a significant price had been paid in terms of output because of faulty sequencing, although most politicians at the time felt that the sequencing was driven by inevitable political processes, which would have been difficult to handle otherwise.

On McKinnon's point that New Zealand had an implicit deposit insurance even though there is no explicit deposit insurance, Brash emphasized that that was certainly true. If banks were registered and supervised as in New Zealand, then there was an implicit deposit insurance. However, he thought that New Zealand's new system reduced the implicit insurance though it certainly did not eliminate it completely. He also noted that when the real-time gross settlements system would have been in place in New Zealand by the third quarter of 1996, the RBNZ would be in a better position to make it unambiguously clear that it would allow a bank to fail.

Brash agreed with McKinnon that the exchange rate, while it was not manipulated in the foreign exchange market, was nevertheless manipulated indirectly through monetary policy. He verified that the exchange rate was a very important transmission mechanism from monetary policy to prices, particularly in a small open economy like New Zealand. He referred to the close similarities between the way the monetary authorities in Singapore and New Zealand handled their exchange rates, since in both countries the exchange rate was an important part of controlling inflation, though the systems he noted were not quite identical.

In particular, Brash agreed with the importance of having strict disclosure and rules related to lending to connected parties as mentioned in the comments of Goldstein. He observed that New Zealand had retained that requirement as one of the very few regulations and rules and he emphasized the importance of having rules to support a disclosure regime. He noted that if a bank in New Zealand were to reveal its capital as being below the 8 percent risk-weighted ratio, the bank was obliged to clearly indicate in the quarterly statement the proposed steps that would be taken to restore the ratio to 8 percent over a very short time period. This represented a tight constraint over banks.

Soedradjad Djiwandono agreed that international cooperation was very important, particularly given the recent rise in the flow of funds between countries in the region. He reported that in November 1995, the monetary authorities in the region had taken initiatives to cooperate with each other. Areas of cooperation discussed, for example, were bilateral agreements among central banks on repurchase agreements. He confirmed, as McKinnon had mentioned, that many Asian countries held US Treasury notes or bills, and it was therefore necessary for them to have a repurchase agreement with each other. He noted that although all the agreements were bilateral (between the central banks), they were making it a regional effort partly to give some kind of message to the players that there was an initiative to cooperate with each other. The initiatives were still not very formal, but he indicated the kind of networking that had been going on. He mentioned that in Indonesia's case, bilateral cooperation between monetary regulators and monetary management had taken place and that Indonesia had bilateral agreements with Malaysia, with Singapore, and with Thailand. Indonesia also had cooperative agreements with Hong Kong in banking supervision, and Indonesia was continuing to strengthen these international initiatives.

On the question of moral suasion, Djiwandono mentioned that Indonesia, in its sequencing of liberalization, was basically moving toward a market economy, and that policy makers understood that issues in the financial sector were increasing in complexity. He noted that the Indonesian authorities were trying to revive and improve all the instruments available. In addition to moral suasion, Indonesia's instruments included open market operations, the discount window, and reserve requirements. He noted that moral suasion was not a substitute for existing formal instruments, but rather a complementary or additional instrument. It was utilized as an instrument partly because the market had not been reacting well to monetary authority guidance, because the players were not fully familiar with the workings of a market system. He noted that more recently, Indonesia had become more eclectic in its reform approach, by taking a gradual approach entailing small steps rather than shock therapy. For a more gradual approach to work, it was necessary to explain the policies very carefully to the players, which was part of the moral suasion. He noted that Indonesia would not use moral suasion as a substitute for any other instrument but as a supplement to be employed until market players became more sophisticated.

Djiwandono agreed with Goldstein's comments on disclosure in areas such as derivatives, but commented that even if there were very clear rules for disclosure, this did not guarantee that things would not go wrong. He said that Indonesia was continually adjusting to such measures, and that disclosure and supervision by the banks themselves (self-regulatory banking) were becoming more and more important, partly because the monetary authority in Indonesia could not reach all the players. He emphasized that it was crucial for market players to have self-regulatory bodies to help ensure that the market worked efficiently.

QUESTIONS FROM THE FLOOR

The **first question** asked was what lessons transition (former command) economies could learn from the different approaches witnessed in Eastern Europe, Latin America, and the experiences in the Asian region, particularly in the PRC. In particular, the questioner asked whether transition economies should follow a commercial banking model or a capital market model, and whether the dominance of commercial banking in the Asian region represented more stability than was being experienced in Eastern Europe where capital markets had been developing rapidly.

Li Ruogu replied that he did not have any solution as to which model the PRC was going to follow. He felt that the PRC could not rely completely on the capital markets which represented direct financing and that at the country's stage of development, it was healthier to concentrate on indirect financing, with commercial banks as the major tools to develop financial services. He noted that as skills and experience accumulated and the capital markets developed, the PRC would certainly move to more direct financing. The PRC's huge demand for funds to support economic development required the growth of capital markets. Li mentioned that the PRC's intention was to gradually develop the capital market, especially given the recent development in the financial markets. However, given the country's present level of technology and information development, it was difficult for the PRC to control, monitor, and supervise activities in capital markets. He noted that the PRC needed a period of learning and accumulating experience before it could move more rapidly toward a market-oriented financial system.

Roberto de Ocampo observed that the PRC was a case study of a country starting from scratch and moving away from a centralized system toward a totally different system. He felt the reforms were proceeding as fast as possible by putting up cautionary signs about building up the new system without immediately destroying everything in the old system. He contrasted this approach with the evidence from some other centrally planned economies, which were transitioning by means of a big bang and the result was a big bang. He felt that those who were impatient about reform in the PRC, or who wanted to see a faster pace of reform failed to appreciate that such a vast country had been able to move so far in its transition. He agreed with Li that the PRC was transitioning as fast as it could and at the same time doing it relatively smoothly and contributing to the growth of wealth in the world. De Ocampo felt that it was instructive to observe the PRC's reform approach and that the path chosen was preferable to the PRC draining the resources of the world in its attempt to move from one system to another.

Paul Dickie noted that ADB was examining the question of whether to use the banking sector model or capital markets model with regard to ADB's support to Mongolia's financial sector development. He had come to the conclusion that at the beginning of financial market development the role of the commercial banks was very important. Assessing credits in the corporate sector and administering and monitoring the corporate performance in relationship to loans could only be done initially by the commercial banks. The main reason for this was that institutional support systems for information, such as credit rating agencies that are needed for capital markets to grow, were not developed in countries at the initial stages of financial sector development. In line with this, he agreed with Li that commercial banks play an important role during the initial period of reforms.

Dickie also commented that from his observations, as financial sectors developed, the nonbank financial institutions took over a majority of the financial assets because they were simply more competitive than commercial banks, with all their brick and mortar and other high costs.

The **second question** focused on the supervisory role of central banks and the approach that New Zealand was taking in this regard. In this context, the questioner asked how relevant moving toward more disclosure (an approach that presupposed a very informed and enlightened public) would be in most parts of Asia, where the public was not so well-educated and enlightened and consequently not very informed about the safety regulations for the banking system.

In reply, Morris Goldstein stated that it obviously helped for the public to know more about banking. However, in most plans for greater disclosure, the authorities did not expect the public to go through the bank records trying to figure out each bank's exposure. He believed that institutions, such as credit rating agencies, would evaluate the banks, and noted that one of the aspects of New Zealand's new system was that institutions would have to post a credit rating on the premises. The question really was whether credit rating agencies would be doing a good job in rating the banks. On disclosure, he felt there were two problems. The first concerned the loan book of a bank. On the one hand, the good news was that it did not change very quickly; on the other hand, the bad news was that it was very hard to evaluate loans, especially loans to small businesses. When there were no secondary market loans, which was the case in most emerging economies, it was hard to obtain information, since secondary markets usually provide information. Second, on the trading book of a bank, he felt that to the extent that the bank was involved in proprietary trading, the good news was that the trading book was easy to evaluate because it recorded market prices. The bad news was that the trading book could change very quickly. A disclosure statement on a bank's trading exposure that was three weeks old would not tell much if that morning one of the traders had decided to increase the bank's exposure on a particular currency and lost the lot. There would be no way of evaluating that activity. Therefore, quality judgment about the bank's internal risk management would be essential. However, Goldstein did not think it would be required for the general public to be able to work their way through banking accounts, but rather, the need was for some general filtered information.

Roberto de Ocampo commented that he didn't think that Brash had made his presentation with a view to suggesting that all the Asian emerging economies should start doing exactly what New Zealand had done. Nevertheless, he felt that countries could learn from New Zealand's experience when starting and continuing with their reform processes, and could move toward doing something similar. He felt that it would be a sad commentary if the process of gradualism was used as an excuse not to be able to move on fronts that are quite useful.

For the **third question,** Morris Goldstein was asked what, in the light of his comments on moral hazard, he thought about the wisdom of creating an international bailout fund to prevent the recurrence of a Mexico-type crisis in the future.

Goldstein commented that discussions had been going on about increasing the size of the General Agreements to Borrow (GAB), which was a line of credit from the G10 countries to the IMF to deal with systemic issues. He felt that one way to reduce the moral hazard problem could be to place a cost on the borrower or lender that tended to offset the subsidy. The inherent subsidy would come about through the use of the facility, and he felt that any discussions about expanding the facility as a way to handle future "Mexicos" would also involve strict policy conditionality. That may tend to reduce the moral hazard. He noted that it would be a scheme similar to coinsurance or to a deductible. However, he noted that there was no doubt that this would pose a trade-off in the sense that there might be rare instances of disturbances of a cross-national nature that could be larger than the capacity of an individual central bank or even of a regional association to deal with. Should a facility be created, it would have to deal with this problem, minimize the spillover effects, and make a sharp reduction in absorption less necessary. (Mexico experienced a drop in GNP of about 7 percent in 1995 and this drop would have been far higher had there been no official loan.) But at the same time that this is done, even with policy conditionality, there are still chances that moral hazard would increase as creditors might not monitor the situation as carefully as they would have done otherwise. In the end, doubling the GAB, with strict conditionality, and provided it is not done too often, is, on balance, a good thing, though he admitted that there are definitely trade-offs involved.

FitzGerald commented that it was known from economic theory and economic practice that markets did not clear by interest rates, but rather by some kind of asset rationing or portfolio decisions based on expectations. So even without any government interference, financial markets were in a constant state of disequilibrium or rationing. Borrowers would always want to borrow more than what was actually available through loans, and that put an enormous onus on lenders (who really make the decisions), rather than on the borrowers. In this context, he noted that a central bank at a national level usually tried to regulate lenders, not borrowers. In other words, central banks penalize lenders for making bad loans, rather than penalizing corporations for borrowing too much. He observed that, at the international level, the reverse position was taken, i.e., the problem lay in Mexico and something had to be done about the borrower rather than about imprudent lending to Mexico. He noted that the bailout operation was also a bailout of the lenders, and this led to the question of whether, internationally, an IMF-style massive intervention on that scale was wise, or whether a BIS-type of route involving coordinated prudential regulation of lenders to maintain the payments system might be more suitable.

CHAPTER EIGHT

CONCLUSIONS AND SUMMING-UP

ROBERTO DE OCAMPO

Chairman de Ocampo noted from the reaction of the audience that it had been a very successful seminar with interesting subject matter, excellent papers, and an enlightening discussion. In his summing-up, he noted that financial sectors in Asia were in transition to, as all papers indicated, a much more market-based system. He noted that there was uniformity in the papers in talking about bank deregulation, capital market development, expansion of the role of the stock exchanges, the movement of the fiscal situation from predominantly one of deficit to one of surplus, the mobilization of domestic savings rate, and the role of international financial flows. He felt that all those topics had been examined very thoroughly and openly by the country presentations, which had described not just a litany of successes, but also showed the positive and negative aspects of reform, and the challenges confronted by countries during the reform process.

An important question which had been addressed was "who is transitioning?" He noted that because much of the focus was on countries, it would seem that only countries were transitioning. He emphasized, however, that it was not just individual countries that were in transition. Countries, the global financial sector, and the private sector were all in transition, and the whole phenomenon of capital flows was transitional and the adjustments that countries were making to it were also part of that transition.

Furthermore, de Ocampo submitted that multilateral institutions, such as the Asian Development Bank, were also in the process of transition.

He questioned what this transitioning meant in light of the presentations in the seminar. For the countries that had made their presentations of transitioning, he felt that the basic philosophy with their transition, or reform, was that they were trying to do it in the context of the creation of wealth, rather than the provisioning of welfare. This was a particularly important point made in the presentations of both the PRC and Indonesia, though not so much in the New Zealand presentation, given that New Zealand is already a wealthy country. He felt that it was an important point to make because of the serious need for policy makers to maintain a balance between providing reform, watching the timing of that reform, and ensuring that reforms benefited the people. In defining the benefit to the people, de Ocampo pointed to domestic views that were not easy to eradicate, such as continued protectionism, leanings toward populism, and the temptation to go for the short term rather than the long term. He considered that a balancing act was necessary and that this had been reflected in the views of the speakers who indicated the need for gradual approaches to reform in order to put in place a system that would take root. However, he also felt that the seminar had come up with an admonition that such gradualism should not be an excuse for foot dragging and that such gradualism should not lead toward a reimposition of the kinds of systems that countries were trying to get away from.

Countries were adjusting to, and reforming for, global competitiveness, de Ocampo observed. He certainly got the impression that there was a consensus on the view that there could be no substitute for sound economic policies. However, he cautioned that such a view must not be reduced to platitudes or the easy use of phrases such as lower inflation rates, or tax reform, but should be brought all the way down to the micro level as Goldstein had advocated. For example, it would not be enough for a country to say that it was going to undertake a financial reform. A country must be very careful that, in reforming, it strengthens its institutions at the micro level, particularly, for example, banking institutions. Therefore, in the reform process, countries must not think that there is a magic wand or a solution that can solve everything simultaneously. He commented on a point made by Djiwandono that the reform process is in constant evolution, and that the monitoring of what is taking place is important in order to make the process as smooth and responsive as possible. That point of view was compared with the experiences of other countries that had been discussed earlier in the seminar, such as those of Eastern Europe and some parts of Latin America. De Ocampo considered Djiwandono's comments to be especially important in the face of large capital flows, which could have either a positive or a negative effect.

The Chairman referred to the important point that, regardless of how reforms in Asia proceeded, the financial requirements of the region's emerging economies were going to be vast. For infrastructure alone, there would be tremendous financial transitioning problems as well as opportunities. Commenting on the private sector and the global financial community, he felt that it was reassuring to see that the Asian region remained committed to a financial reform agenda that was continuing to move toward market-based operations. The only differences among reforming countries seemed to be *where* the launching pad was located and he noted in this context that the PRC was starting from scratch, whereas New Zealand had already achieved a market-based system. He considered that there was a need to appreciate the differences in the types of economies and where they were with respect to the reform process, while at the same time appreciating that they were all moving toward market-based systems. He emphasized that failure to realize those differences could lead to private capital flows being misdirected. However, he noted that all the presentations were equally radical depending on where they were coming from. New Zealand's move toward self-regulation was no less radical than the PRC's move to almost totally revamp its banking system, or Indonesia's move away from being entirely dependent on oil.

De Ocampo emphasized the need for the private sector to exercise creativity in the face of this transition and stressed that the future financial needs would be vast. He said that the Philippines realized that those needs were going to be very large and that meeting infrastructure requirements would require a balancing act between the rate of return demanded by the private sector as against the types of rates, fees, charges, toll rates, etc., that would be acceptable to the final beneficiaries. A balancing act and creativity from the private sector capital markets in coming up with the appropriate instruments would be required.

The role for multilateral institutions like the ADB might, among other things, be to help enlighten the global community on the various transitions taking place and to provide documentation of the lessons that could be learned, not only from the Asian region but also from around the world. De Ocampo believed that the ADB could assist in financial sector liberalization through providing support for the development of appropriate mechanisms at the micro level along the lines that the discussants had indicated. He emphasized that such assistance would ensure that a country's transition did not get out of hand, and it would also help ensure the necessary public support for reforms. He noted that this would, of course, require an understanding of the situation of each country and the ADB could pursue a devil's advocate role to encourage countries to continually think about the various lessons to be learned from others, as well as about the improvements that needed to be made.

In conclusion, de Ocampo noted that valuable lessons had been learned during the seminar. He thanked all the participants and those who had presented papers. He also thanked the discussants for adding material substantive elements to the discussion from which all the participants could learn. He hoped that the papers would be made available in print, so that countries could derive further benefit from the proceedings. Finally, he thanked the ADB for providing a forum for the exchange of views on financial reform in Asia, and for the ADB's continued support to the region's financial development and overall economic growth and stability.